April 6, 1993

Celi

Gruwell

Mothering

BOOKS AUTHORED OR CO-AUTHORED
BY ELAINE CANNON

Adversity

As a Woman Thinketh

Baptized and Confirmed: Your Lifeline to Heaven

Be a Bell Ringer

Bedtime Stories for Grownups

Boy of the Land, Man of the Lord

Called to Serve Him

Corner on Youth

Eight Is Great

The Girl's Book

God Bless the Sick and Afflicted

Heart to Heart

Life—One to a Customer

Love You

Merry, Merry Christmases

The Mighty Change

Mothers and "Other Mothers"

Not Just Ordinary Young Men and Young Women

Notable Quotables

Putting Life in Your Life Story

Quote Unquote

The Seasoning

The Summer of My Content

The Time of Your Life

Turning Twelve or More: Living by the Articles of Faith

Mothering

ELAINE CANNON

BOOKCRAFT
Salt Lake City, Utah

Library of Congress Catalog Card Number: 93-70471
ISBN 0-88494-872-2

First Printing, 1993

Printed in the United States of America

Contents

Mothering is the best thing to happen to anyone. It is awesome to have that little person's hand in yours and become aware that his or her life is in your hands as well. Whatever the day's struggles, when the child is tucked in bed at last, his or her smile is worth it.

To remember one's own mother daily, even in small ways, is to reap such richness of soul and gratitude of heart as to be almost unbelievable. It is to note her inimitableness in one's life. To think about Mother is to be flooded with a feeling—second only to love of God—of eternal affection for one's own mother. No matter what the years have or have not brought.

The Lord and his prophets give scriptural support to the majesty of your role in life, Mother! In addition, the mother of Joseph Smith; Hannah, mother of Samuel; Emma Ray, wife of President David O. McKay; and Mrs. Elizabeth Stanton, 1860 suffragette, proclaim the holy charge of women. They speak from personal experience. Even though every mother won't nurture a son who grows up famous, always remember that what you are doing is very holy business. You are in partnership with God for the well-being of his spirit children while they're taking their turn on earth. So take heart, Mother!

Mothering is God's way of blessing the world. Women who play the loving, protective part with infants and children, with handicapped people and needful seniors deserve a tribute. Mothers who deal with tough problems of their own prove skillful in helping other women in the challenging role of mothering. As for the rest of us, we are constantly amazed at how those who have paved the way for us remain a part of us forever. The touching stories included here are taken from real-life happenings.

Mother and Other Mothers 41

To women who have the selfless strength to wait upon, to yearn after, to care for, and to love someone else's birth child goes the highest praise. Ah, now there is first-rate mothering! Here are perspectives and stories about women who have done just that for a season or a lifetime. What are the hazards in such an opportunity? What are the blessings? And how should a girl feel who, because of untimely, illegitimate motherhood, puts her child into the hands of an "other mother"?

Mother: An Example of the Believer 51

Being a mother and being an example of the believer seem to be synonymous at first thought. But this isn't necessarily true. Everyone loves her own mother, but not every mother has equally sturdy fortitude about gospel principles. Mothers usually believe in God because they've had a miracle at his hands. But to believe in God is not the same as believing what God commands or teaches or explains. One of the several examples of believers included in this chapter is Flora Amussen Benson, wife of President Ezra Taft Benson. Insightful excerpts from her funeral in August 1992 illustrate her righteous influence as one who lived as she believed.

Mother: The Proceedings in Her Days 61

Where does peace on earth begin? In the home. Where do women learn Christlike patience and contentment—anyway? In the home. Where do we learn to love an enemy? Where do children learn about the value of human life, the dignity that should surround procreation? Where do they come to truly understand the meaning behind the song, "I Am a Child of God"? With a caring mother such understanding can come. And if the mother in such a home keeps a record of the proceedings in her days, that influence can carry into succeeding generations. Sometimes a family member who can't be reached in any other way will be touched by the personal records of Mother. Perhaps another verse of "I Am a Child of God" should be written to remind us that—
> *Children of God are we.*
> *We love him faithfully,*
> *And he loves everyone of us—*
> *He helps us patiently.*

and styles. No doubt about it, remembering Mother is a good thing to do!

I am the poet of the woman
the same as the man,
And I say it is as great to be
a woman as to be a man,
And I say there is nothing
greater than the mother
of men.

—Walt Whitman

Acknowledgments

Gratitude is a remembrance of the heart.
—Robert Louis Stevenson

Gratitude is a softening of the heart and an awakening of the mind regarding the skill, the kindness, and the necessary help in completing such a project as this. There are many to thank, and surely they know who they are and the warm appreciation their names evoke.

Almost everyone has an opinion about motherhood, and some are especially suitable to the purpose of this book. Appreciation must go to many for their input, expertise, ideas, research, and creative expression—published or unhearalded.

Mother: Look at You!

What feeling is so nice as a child's hand in yours?
—Marjorie Holmes

Mothering is the best thing to happen to anyone. It is awesome to press a little person's hand in yours with the awareness that his or her life is in your control as well. There swells in you a mix of tenderness and something akin to fear. Prayers come easily in such a mood.

Prayers of gratitude for such a privilege as mothering affords.

There is another truth about mothering: when the child is tucked in bed at last—with the hassle of care and cleanup, delay and discipline over for a time—the smile flashed your way makes the effort worth it all. Or a letter comes from your missionary so joyfully wired now that he gently suggests repentance for the family. And you are satisfied. And instead of wanting to give up you want to get better at it!

Look at you . . . singing away with the sisters, "Lord, make me a channel of thy peace!" The words may be St. Francis of Assisi's, but they are the focus of a mothering woman's heart.

Lord, make me a channel of thy peace
That where there is hatred I may bring love,
That where there is wrong I may bring the spirit of forgiveness,
That where there is discord I may bring harmony,

That where there is error I may bring truth,
That where there is doubt I may bring faith,
That where there is despair I may bring hope,
That where there are shadows I may bring thy light,
That where there is sadness I may bring joy.
Lord, grant that I may seek rather
To comfort—than to be comforted;
To understand—than to be understood;
To love—than to be loved;
For it is by giving that one receives;
It is by self-forgetting that one finds;
It is by forgiving that one is forgiven;
It is by dying that one awakens to eternal life.

This is a Mother's Day song, all right, and since mothers are in style every day of every month of the lifetimes under their wing, mothers need such a golden goal. It is an old poem—God inspired, no doubt. It is a familiar song. It is time worn and proven by mothers. It is therefore perfect for a tribute to the absolute oldest and most noble profession and possibility for women.

God has revealed the divinely appointed opportunities for women. No matter how the world carries on—demeaning women, exploiting their beauty and promise, keeping them chattels and slaves, expecting them to single-handedly carry the burdens of parenting in any situation (divorced, widowed, unwed, unequally yoked, working inside and outside the home, supporting a big-deal husband as his hostess as well as wife)—no matter, God gave to woman to be his arm of love. To men God gave his arm of leadership. And God gives no assignment or commandment without providing a way for it to be accomplished. Woman's mothering role, her servant status, can be a blight or a blessing.

But look at you! Carrying on! Counting your blessings, doing your remarkable thing. Remembering that bedtime smile of the loving, needful, grateful child. Conducting family prayers, if need be. Forgiving and loving—even mothering your male family members *anyway! Your* own heart, you see, is warmed and filled by the Holy Spirit.

When we come to understand and obey the gospel of Jesus Christ and the whole exquisite plan of life, we will know that God established the difference in the roles of men and women so that it is not possible for one to be exalted without the other. Some of a mothering woman's divinely appointed opportunities include:

- becoming a partner with God in mothering his earth children
- training up a child in the way he or she should grow
- nudging and nurturing a man to goodness and godliness
- cultivating a woman's unique qualities to discern, intuit, comfort, stand by
- preparing herself in all ways to fill such a lofty place in the eternal scheme of things
- seeking wisdom from the scriptures and the prophets
- seeking learning from the schools of life through books, courses, people
- experimenting upon the word of God, which encompasses all truth wherever it is found
- moving forward, personally progressing as well as to enrich and control one's life

Eliza R. Snow said, "Let the women seek for wisdom instead of power and they will have all the power they have wisdom to exercise."

My own point of view is that there are two important days in a woman's life: the day she is born and the day she finds out why. For me no day in my life can top the day my first baby was brought to me in the hospital—newborn, fresh from heaven, an incredibly lovely miracle. For this I was born. And as each succeeding newborn came there was a replay of the miracle that lifted my inner heart to its highest. Oh, just imagine the blight on a career lady's life if she were to wake up one morning and remember that she forgot to have children. So much for cramming your life full of nonessentials.

When we do take up the flame of mothering, what is it we are supposed to do, what are we supposed to be like, how shall we nurture? What is it we wish we had as mothers to impart to our children? How we feel about those we mother proves interesting with a closer look. At our house we built up our four daughters, we considered them very special—little princesses. Juliana, princess of the Netherlands, on the other hand, proclaimed, "Our child will not be raised in tissue paper! . . . We don't want her to even hear the word *princess*."

People growing up in this, a hostile world, need a very reaching, profound kind of loving and reassurance, steady tenderness, wisdom in guidance even more than knowledge. Then one day comes the difficult education—the loosening of the ties so carefully put in place in the beginning. For we rear those we mother to move forward, knowing they really won't look back until they are parents themselves and begin to understand.

Consider these remarkable examples of mothering from our sisters in the scriptures:

Eve. He called her Eve because she was the "mother of all living." She was Adam's helpmeet, not just a partner to keep a man from being lonely. As the proper definition of the word reveals, God gave Adam a "helper worthy of him."

Sarah. Now, here is the prime model of faith in God and in his servants. She became a mother after the time of women was done and was the absolute epitome of a noble wife and mother.

Mary. Handmaiden of God. Mother of Jesus. Especially read Luke and Matthew for insights on this inimitable mother. May we never forget her prime example.

Dorcas. She mothered mothers. Her "almsdeeds" were so healing that when she died the widows wept for her, and when Peter arrived in her city he returned her to life.

Sariah. She clearly loved her sons and was concerned for their welfare. Upon their return after obtaining the plates of brass, she rejoiced and bore testimony that the Lord had protected her sons.

It is difficult for a woman to perfect herself in the confusion of today's world. There is an even greater challenge to achieve perfection as we match wits in the relationships that mothering imposes.

But look at you, Mother! Not only are you making it work, you are making it wonderful. This is the grandness of mothering. It is the best thing to happen to anyone!

Mother, you are an unforgettable woman. A person who receives a mother's unconditional, unequivocal love knows this. Mothers are so important we simply cannot forget them. What is more, we choose to remember them all the rest of our lives.

This book, *Mothering,* has been prepared as a tribute to all who mother!

Mother Dear, I Love You So!

I would weave you a song, my Mother.
—Madelaine Mason-Manheim

To watch a young mother proudly herd her little ones about while toting all the accompanying equipment is to note her liveliness.

To marvel at a woman whose life is happily cumbered with much serving among her family, groups, causes, household tasks, and professional pressures is to note her worthiness.

To meet a gracious older woman, one with the natural beauty of living in love and investing herself in others is to note her loveliness.

To remember one's own mother daily in small ways is to note her inimitableness and reap richness and gratitude.

To open one's heart to such mothers is to be flooded with a feeling second only to the love of God. Mothers dear, we love you so. All of you!

Within the great tapestry of mankind is the awesome corner that is largely our own family—intricate threads spun by mother and father, brothers, sisters, aunts, teachers, grandparents, and generations of genes and influences. We honor God's plan of families and the understanding that we have of our kindred—dead or alive: we are part of them, and they are part of us for all the days of our lives.

It goes without saying that mothers usually have to put aside some personal development and pleasure for childbirth, child care, older parent care, and household upkeep. Oh, we know there are dysfunctional families, heartbreaks, children with mix-match parents, homeless loved ones and strangers, addicts, abusers, sinners, helpless victims, and physically and emotionally starving humans . . . we know! But for right now we will think of the happy, we will look to goodness and the ideal, we will praise the struggling, serving, charming, lovely mothers of all ages.

We think of Mother at unexpected times, in quaint places, under dire circumstances. We lean toward that haven when we are threatened—even trembling with age.

We hear an old adage, see a sibling's leg bounce in a certain way in time with some music, find a tarnished, initialed silver spoon, and Mother comes to mind. The nostalgic fragrance of her being and her spirit is suddenly fresh again.

Punch the right key, and Mother, long gone, plays on our consciousness in a moving melody of safeness and goodness. Suddenly she is reborn in the heart as a fountainhead of truth! of joy! of wholesomeness! of endurance! of ingenuity! of forgiveness! of love! of awareness! and (oh, for goodness' sake, admit it now) of wisdom—the daily, straightforward wisdom of the Gods! You find your soul paying homage to such motherly wisdom as "Each night one gets ready for the next day." "Each Saturday one prepares for the Sabbath." "Repentance, prayer, and pleading are part of the schedule."

Margaret Mead, a famous anthropologist, ethnologist, writer, and teacher, wrote of her relationship with her mother in her auto-biography, *Blackberry Winter: My Earlier Years*. She speaks lovingly of her mother's influence on her.

Before my birth, my mother kept a little notebook in which she jotted down, among other things, quotations from William James about developing all of a child's senses, as well as the titles of articles on which she was working for various encyclopedias, and here she wrote, "When I knew baby was coming I was anxious to do the best for it."

Pictures of me as a baby show me in the arms of my mother or grandmother, with their hair down and wearing wrappers, dressed in a way I have no memory of seeing either of them. Only now, after so many years, I realize that it was for her children's sake that my mother pinned up her hair so carefully every morning as soon as she got up. . . . In turn, the first thing I do in the morning is to comb my hair, and when my daughter was young I put on something pretty—as I still do when I am staying in a house where there are children. (*Blackberry Winter* [New York: William Morrow & Company, 1972], p. 19.)

Mothers do have a way with them.

Over the years of living and mothering, I've noticed that my heart is a honeycomb. It is riddled with little cells that close away the vital happenings of my life: small celebrations, disappointments, impossible love, a few innocent pleasures that belong only to the childish days when one sees through the glass darkly.

In the season of my maturity I must live with my honeycomb. I even use this imagery deliberately when I don't feel very brave, locking an emotion in its cell after the fashion of Scarlett, who chose to "think about it tomorrow." Now I frequently seal up grief and death, the giving up and the going on.

Writing about my mother requires that I open the honeycomb, that I think back through to my own spirited earthly guardian: back, back, back to the earliest memory of her—buttoned shoes on a patterned floor as she stooped to retrieve my baby bottle that had somehow jumped from my groping fingers . . . again.

As I write, she is a presence in my consciousness and my affections. She is yet a yardstick for evaluation and behavior.

Oh, Mother dear, I love you so.

Some of you will remember a mother's apron, a special æbleskive pan, some kitchen skill. My mother cooked, all right, and our house was the scene of food functions of all kinds, including feeding the Depression Era tramps. We carted casseroles to the sick and afflicted, but they weren't "sacred" or "special" as some claim when doing their good deeds. But then cooking was *not* my mother's life, her red flag of self-esteem. Nonetheless, I learned great food basics from Mother.

I learned to scrape dark toast, turn it upside down, and tap it on the sink edge to release burnt crumbs!

I learned the philosophy of food presentation—almost as

important as flavor! We became adept at making radish roses and candlestick salad (you top a half of a banana with a cherry and poke it into a circle of canned pineapple).

I learned not to serve "naked" food. A bare platter surrounding carved meat, steamed vegetables, or sliced fruit was unthinkable. Dress it with wisps of parsley, mint, or nasturtium leaves. Lettuce, at least!

I learned that paprika was sprinkled "for color" on pears, cottage cheese, deviled eggs, potatoes on the half shell, and baking-powder biscuits smothered with creamed chipped beef.

Some of you will remember a mother's work gloves molded in mud to her cupped hand setting the spring bulbs. Sidonie-Gabrielle Colette wrote of her mother's "radiant garden face, so much more beautiful than her anxious indoor face." I understand that. My mother gardened her worries away, vigorously yanking the June grass from the tangled rock garden out front, pruning the cherry trees marking the back property line, or mulching the floribunda roses. She even wrote a garden column for the *Deseret News* for a time. But my mother was at her radiant best in her book-crammed corner. Here there was an aura about her that was startling. Moving among her variety of books, she became a light herself.

In my mother's study were the workings of her soul—mind-things like reference books, maps, anthologies, a magnifying glass, pencils jammed in a thread box, ruffled pages of mysterious scrawled notes in a lined tablet; tools the body used to enrich the mind and spirit. And whole sets of classic children's literature.

When my mother was mothering, she was so excited whenever she sent one of us to the enormous dictionary to look up a word we didn't know. She would drop whatever she was doing to listen to our findings. Even the beginning readers in our family knew how to use the worn, floppy-covered fat encyclopedic dictionary purchased from a door-to-door salesman in Depression days. Her eyes would snap and sparkle in a lively discussion with us about usage, too—not only correct English but also the right word in the right place to make meaning exact, lovely, moving.

During first grade I started my own fat scrapbooks, sitting beside her and pasting in quotes cut from *Pictorial Magazine, Good Housekeeping, Saturday Evening Post, Liberty,* the *Relief Society Magazine,* and the *Improvement Era.* I even laboriously copied mysterious lines I found underlined in her favorite books. Much,

much later I came to understand and value the meaning of these things.

Of course, we all grew up cherishing words, ideas, philosophies, phrases, and books—even the feel of the binding, the quality of the paper, and the look of the typeface.

For many years, my own mother was the weekly book review hostess for the Lion House on South Temple. When books were delivered from Deseret Book or when the *New York Times Book Review* section came in the mail, Mother hugged them to her. Selected books became burdened with paper clips, abridging a long book into a one-hour unforgettable story. My mother was a storyteller. People gathered about her. I once saw a beautiful piece of native sculpture called *The Storyteller*. It was of an American Indian woman with assorted children clustered about. I think of my mother like that. I remember being spellbound by her "book review books," such as *Child of the Sea*, by Elizabeth Goudge; *Keys of the Kingdom*, by A. J. Cronin; *Magnificent Obsession*, by Lloyd C. Douglas; and Ben Franklin's autobiography. My mother even abridged the biblical history of Paul the Apostle into a near movie script. All with elastics, paper clips, and margin markings slanted in her swift script.

I don't know what leftover deprivation provoked my mother's devotion to stubby pencils, chewed in her beautiful, flawless teeth never touched by any dentist. These scarred pencils were regularly yet strangely carved into a new point by a paring knife held against the wood and whittled off in a direction away from Mother's determined body. The shavings fell neatly into the toilet to be flushed away.

In fifty years of keeping my home and desk, I never once have flicked paprika on a pure pear (though I recognize my roots for a color consciousness in cooking). I fastidiously avoid chewed stub-pencils. In spite of Mother, or perhaps because of her, I prefer pencils smooth and sleek thanks to a mechanical sharpener and topped with a fresh eraser almost before it's needed.

But, Mother dear, I loved you, so I noticed your ways and rituals all along; though I don't whittle pencil points, I bask yet in all the practical instructions that I received from you—in your ingenuity and resourcefulness. I tenderly remember what you awakened within me. I think about the horizons revealed in the thirst for learning the gospel, the love of words and books and *people*.

My mother noticed that people talked a lot about free agency, even back then! She observed that people should learn correct principles *before* they tried to govern themselves, to have their own way. Everything, everything, everything in our lives, our home, our adventures, our relationships, our worship or celebrations, our despair—everything had a lesson in it that my mother inevitably and emphatically pointed out to us. Such lessons we were not allowed to discover for ourselves, because we might miss some practical perspective about living life.

I have a valued friend who all his years has taken appropriate occasion to repeat, "My widowed mother gave us all that money could not buy." My mother gave us precious education that schools could not. Practical stuff as well as valuable truth based firmly on eternal gospel principles, such as: God lives whether people believe it or not. Jesus is our friend and redeemer whether people choose to serve him or not. Of course, we were not allowed to sin or all the angels would make note of it and our day of being encircled in God's arms would certainly be delayed if not in jeopardy.

Because there wasn't a meetinghouse close by, my mother held religion classes in our garage. When the new chapel was finished, my mother provided the home-baked bread for the sacrament and the stage furnishings for the one-act plays. God was to be worshiped and obeyed, and life was to be lived. She taught us by word and example how to find the lessons and how to pass them on.

In my mother's last years she followed a daily ritual of reading a bit from four categories: the scriptures, a book on medicine, a current events publication, and classic literature. Balanced study, she called it. Still we learned from her: the glory of God is intelligence, and whatever principle of intelligence a person attains in this life will be his eternally. What a valuable example!

In Singapore, the cultural tradition has long been for a bride to present her mother with a decorated basket filled with gifts she has learned in her mother's home: a bit of handwork, a thing of beauty, a delicate morsel, paintings or poetry, a symbolic witness of God. I was honored with such a basket when I visited there. It was given to me by the Young Women. I loved the gift, but I wept later because I hadn't known of such a charming custom when my own mother was still alive. She gave me too much for a basket, but with a honeycomb heart everything can fit in!

JoAnn R. Barwick, editor of *House Beautiful,* wrote at Christmastime about the importance of home and families. A successful professional in her field, she says, "Christmas is a great simplifier. When I gather with my family at Christmas, I'm no longer a magazine editor, but mother, wife, and daughter. No matter what other hats we wear in life, at Christmas we automatically assume our family roles, continuing the old traditions and creating new memories for our own children."

Keeping traditions, however, does not absolutely ensure a merry time at Christmas, and neither does just having children a mother make. A woman must work at that. That was the way of it with my mother, so how could I feel otherwise?

Oh, Mother dear, I love you so! All I could really hope or want for my own children is that they love me as I love you and as we both have always loved Heavenly Father.

Mother: Her Holy Charge

I say to mothers what a holy charge is theirs—with what
a kingly power their love might rule the fountains of the
new-born mind.
                              —Lydia Huntly Segourney

Just as life is more than we know, so are the newborn spirits that
come under the care of mothers, who have paid a price of some
kind for the privilege and joy of relating to their babies—naturally
born or adopted by love or assignment.

In a stirring address delivered at the tenth National Woman's
Rights Convention in New York in 1860, Mrs. Elizabeth Stanton
stated the role of women emphatically: "If in marriage either party
claims the right to stand supreme, to woman, the mother of the
race, belongs the scepter and the crown. Her life is one long sacrifice for man. You tell us that among womankind there is no
Moses, Christ, or Paul—no Michelangelo, Beethoven, Shake-
speare—no Columbus or Galileo—no Locke or Bacon. Behold
those mighty minds so grand, so comprehensive—they themselves
are *our* great works! Into you, O sons of the earth, goes all of us
that is immortal. In you center our very life, our hopes, our intens-
est love. For you we gladly pour out our hearts' blood and die,
knowing that from our suffering comes forth a new and more glorious resurrection of thought and life."

We give thanks for the privilege of participating in the gift of
life, of mothering with the holy charge in mind and heart. We give
thanks, as well, for the blessing of being a partner with God. We

witness to the awesome responsibility of mothering and to the sanctity of family life.

Home is the best place in the world to teach the loftiest ideal and to provide opportunities for its application in social and political life—perfect liberty of action as long as one does not trespass on the rights of others. The Lord placed this divinely appointed responsibility of teaching exactly where it belongs: "Inasmuch as parents have children in Zion, or in any of her stakes which are organized, that teach them not to understand the doctrine of repentance, faith in Christ the Son of the living God, and of baptism and the gift of the Holy Ghost . . . , the sin be upon the heads of the parents. . . . They shall also teach their children to pray, and to walk uprightly before the Lord." (D&C 68:25, 28.)

Motherhood was a favorite topic of President David O. McKay. In emphasizing woman's holy charge, he once said, "Mother performs the greatest duty in all the world. I think it was Napolean who once was asked what was the greatest need in the world and he answered, 'Mother! That is all.'"

Studying the history of mankind and watching life unfold, observing the themes of general conference over the years as the Brethren admonish the Saints, and learning from our own experiences, we can come to a wonderful awareness that a mother is far more than a one-woman brigade to dispense love pats, orange juice, and clean diapers. She is always with us.

Home is where people start from, and the starting is immediate! We can find a remarkable reminder of this in the following excerpts from a poem by Walt Whitman:

> There was a child went forth every day,
> And the first object he look'd upon,
>   that object he became,
> And that object became part of him for the day
>   or a certain part of the day,
> Or for many years or stretching cycles of years. . . .
>
> His own parents, he that had father'd him and she
>   that had conceiv'd him in her womb
>   and birth'd him,
> They gave this child more of themselves than that,
> They gave him afterward every day,
>   they became part of him. . . .

> The family usages, the language, the company,
>> the furniture, the yearning and swelling heart,
> Affection that will not be gainsay'd, the sense
>> of what is real. . . .
> The streets themselves and the facades of houses,
>> and goods . . .
> These became part of that child who went forth
>> every day . . .

Consider the following letter written by a sensitive man who supports the role of mother. With the author's permission, Elder M. Russell Ballard shared it with the world during his address at the October 1992 general conference:

> I was born into the Church and was taught the gospel at my mother's knee. Through her diligence and perseverance, she kindled a small ember of testimony that never left me even through some of the roughest times of my life. In my teen years Satan hit me hard. It was during the late 1960s and early 1970s, a time of great turmoil, and Satan was hard at work on me. I was taken with the practice of free drugs, free love, free fun, and the rest of the world be damned. Beginning with my first drink of alcohol, I began to slowly deteriorate. After alcohol, other drugs were that much easier to use. In order to take drugs, you must become a good liar. You learn to do whatever it takes to conceal your behavior from others.
>
> After many years of living this way, all my moral fiber seemed to be completely eroded away. I had a minimal amount of conscience and had sunk to the depths of despair and depression. I watched friends die from drugs and suicide. As time passed, my friends and I were exposed to the criminal justice system. In fact, many of my former friends are still in prison. Had it not been for the small flicker of testimony instilled in me by my mother when I was a child, to know that Heavenly Father could still love me, I have reservations as to whether I would even be writing this letter today. (Quoted in M. Russell Ballard, "The Joy of Hope Fulfilled," *Ensign*, November 1992, p. 32.)

The mother of this man never gave up on him. She believed that if he turned to the Lord, he would make it back. Family and

friends supported him, loved him, and reminded him of the goodness of God and the truth of the gospel. Eventually he did come to
himself—his best self—as a useful citizen and disciple of Christ.

Joseph Smith often praised his mother for his training. He
said, "Blessed is my mother, for her soul is ever filled with benevo-
lence and philanthropy." It was highly touching to spectators to
see Joseph reach out frantically to put his hand through the wagon
canvas to hold his mother's hand before he was hauled away to
prison in 1838. According to an account by Leonard J. Arrington,
director of the Joseph Fielding Smith Institute of History at Brigham Young University, Joseph's mother was the principal model
for Mormon women in the years following the murder of her son
and Prophet of The Church of Jesus Christ of Latter-day Saints:

> At a conference of the Church held in Nauvoo Oct. 8, 1845,
> "Mother" Smith, as she was referred to, was called upon to
> speak and made the following remarks:
> "I raised up 11 children, 7 boys. I raised them in the fear
> of God. When they were 2 or 3 years old I told them I wanted
> them to love God with all their hearts. I told them to do good.
> I want all of you to do the same. God gives us children and we
> are accountable. . . . Remember that I love children, young
> folks, and everybody. . . . I call you brothers and sisters and
> children. If you consider me a Mother in Israel, I want you to
> say so."
> According to the minutes, Brigham Young then arose and
> said, "all who consider Mother Smith as a Mother in Israel,
> signify it by saying yes." There were loud shouts of yes, ac-
> cording to the clerk. A Mother in Israel was a title of honor,
> given to the most exemplary women in ancient Israel and in
> the early Church. (*Church News,* 5 May 1985.)

The Prophet Joseph's mother taught him to search the scriptures. When he was just fourteen, he was studying the Bible for
answers. He read James 1:5 and then applied it to his problem of
which church he should join. He asked of God, and the answer to
his prayer changed the world forever.

For example, Sister Emma Ray McKay, wife of President David
O. McKay, won hearts in her day responding to calls to preach and

teach around the Church as she accompanied her husband. One of her most oft-quoted statements is still relevant today because it is true: "If there is righteousness in the heart, there will be beauty in the character. If there is beauty in the character, there will be harmony in the home. If there is harmony in the home, there will be order in the nation. If there is order in the nation, there will be peace in the world."

Never underestimate the power of a mother, for hers is the power to turn a life around, to survive terrible tragedy and leave her mark of goodness and faith as an example to all, to so rear her family that the pattern of outcome described by Sister McKay will, in fact, come to pass.

The Old Testament story of Hannah, mother of Samuel, must leave today's mother marveling. Yet here is a story somewhat like Mary's, mother of Jesus, and Lucy Mack's, mother of the Prophet Joseph. Each story involves the sacred law of sacrifice before God and the lasting influence of mothers upon sons.

Hannah's requirements would sorely test any woman of any age. In today's world particularly there are good women who would marvel about this devoted woman. Many of our good women today find themselves unable to bear children—like Hannah. The story of Hannah and her young son is briefly recorded in the first three chapters of the book of 1 Samuel, named after Hannah's son. Oh, it is worth reading, worth the study time of any woman.

The record describes Hannah's grief at not having a child. She couldn't eat. She wept. She was in "bitterness of soul." Her husband loved her deeply and asked her, "Why weepest thou? and why eatest thou not? and why is thy heart grieved? am I not better to thee than ten sons?"

But Hannah had vowed a vow that if the Lord would open her womb and give her a son, she would give him over to the Lord.

And the Lord remembered Hannah and answered her prayers, and she bore a son whose name was Samuel. This courageous woman had the joy of caring for Samuel until he was a young boy. Then one day Hannah gathered certain needful things and took Samuel with her to the house of the Lord in Shiloh. She stood before the priest Eli and said, "O my lord, as thy soul liveth, my lord, I am the woman that stood by thee here, praying unto the

Lord. For this child I prayed; and the Lord hath given me my petition which I asked of him: therefore also I have lent him to the Lord; as long as he liveth he shall be lent to the Lord."

Mother Hannah made Samuel a "little coat" and brought it to him year after year when she came with her husband to offer the yearly sacrifice. Samuel grew and the Lord was with him: "all Israel from Dan even to Beer-sheba knew that Samuel was established to be a prophet of the Lord. And . . . the Lord revealed himself to Samuel."

Does a mother have a holy charge? Are there happy endings for the mothers who rear their children up in righteousness, giving them to God in the ways he has decreed?

Sister Barbara Winder mothered her own beloved family of children and then became national president for Lambda Delta Sigma, the Church's sorority for college-aged women. She served as general president of the Relief Society for several years and has been a mission mother twice. She understands the holy charge of women to be God's partner in teaching his spirit children the things they need to get back into his presence one day. She shared the following personal experience with me especially for this book:

"It was nearing the Christmas season. We would be in San Diego away from family and loved ones as my husband was serving as mission president there. My heart was yearning homeward. What kind of remembrance could I send the grandchildren to help them know how precious they are? I looked at the LDS bookstore, browsing through stuffed animals and storybooks but not finding the answer to my quest. I was about to leave when I noticed a little gold chain with the words "I Am a Child of God." Perfect for the granddaughters! What about the grandsons? The lady in the shop showed me little gold tie tacs with the exact same words.

"Excitedly I shared my feelings with her. 'I want the grandchildren to know who they are. These will be perfect.'

"'Yes,' she said, 'and it will be a good reminder for their mothers, as well.'"

Being treated with love and respect is certainly one of the secrets to helping children remember who they are and to increasing their self-respect. Remembering who these children are should increase the quality of our nurturing care.

How can one who is a mothering angel before God help a child learn sacred truths? What should she teach?

She will teach repentance, faith, baptism, and the gift of the Holy Ghost. She will teach the value of this gift and explain how the Holy Ghost can bless their lives. She will be wise to teach virtue, knowledge, temperance, patience, kindness, godliness, charity, humility, honesty, diligence, and, above all, the wide and vital range of love.

Examples of how Mother can fulfill her charge are numerous. Some are included all through this tribute to mothering. Some mothers will find many more examples for themselves. One important key for mothers—indeed, for all parents—is recorded in Moses 6:58–62. God gave to Adam a commandment to teach vital sacred things to Adam's children. The next verses describe the plan and purpose of life, the way to sanctification, the role of the Comforter in their lives, and "the peaceable things of immortal glory; the truth of all things; that which quickeneth all things, which maketh alive all things; that which knoweth all things, and hath all power according to wisdom, mercy, truth, justice, and judgment. . . . This is the plan of salvation unto all men, through the blood of mine Only Begotten."

The motto for Latter-day Saint women charged with the blessed responsibility of mothering might well be "Choose you this day whom ye will serve, . . . but as for me and my house, we will serve the Lord" (Joshua 24:15).

Whether by an act of nature, by choice, or by circumstance, mothers are agents, after all, for Heavenly Father—his angels for a season in helping to bring some peace and joy to others. Their holy charge is to help prepare each child who goes forth.

Mother: God's Blessing

God could not be everywhere, and therefore he made mothers.

—Jewish Proverb

Whatever would we do without mothers? Mothering *is* God's way of blessing the world. One who mothers gives things reminiscent of heaven: heart warmth, security, self-worth, holiness.

A woman should feel that her power is like that which Ruskin says lived in the artist: it is not so much "in them as through them." Mothers are especially good at this. They are busy blessing the world as God's agents in training up children in the way they should go. It is an exquisite assignment in life.

God set up the system of families as the human nest for newcomers. But a mother is more than a married woman with a family or perhaps an unwed teenager with a baby she hadn't planned on and for whom she now is responsible. Schoolteachers, for example, do a kind of mothering and nurturing even though they aren't related to the youngsters. Once on a television talk show, teachers were asked to describe their role in the field of education, to give a job description, if you will. A new kindergarten teacher grandly remarked: "I start four- and five-year-olds on the path of scholarship, leadership, and a lifetime of integrity. I also pour juice."

For a more complete picture, add friendly arms encircling a distressed little human being. What a difference a hug makes! With a special clarity and a tender throb of the heart, each of us can recall this kind of comfort on some needed occasion. Loving mothers of all walks of life leave an indelible mark. Their wisdom seems inspired—often beyond their natural ability. Their platitudes, explanations, and apothegms—all of Mother's Marvelous Maxims are treasures.

Endless outpourings of food, clothing, money, advice, comfort, Band-Aids, and, yes, juice are recalled as love given freely upon request, love unconditional, love when no one else shows it, love when it is deserved least. With her hand in God's, a mother carries the unselfish burden of receiving spirit children of his eternal family and showing them the possibilities a physical body can provide them during their turn on earth.

A mother not only serves Heavenly Father in coaching precious human beings along life's climb but also brings the Father and his Beloved Son right into the picture, thus vividly teaching the reason for living and growing, the promise for future joy, the cause for hope in the midst of life's inevitable struggle and despair.

Frequently even children in trouble—in detention or foster homes, for example—would rather be with their own mother under difficult circumstances than be detained in clean, peaceful facilities. Because of that inimitable tie, mothers are remembered, often beyond their own immediate realm, or in spite of imperfect traits.

A certain funeral was under way for the mother of five young children. She had taken her own life in a way that broke the hearts of her family and set the neighbors gossiping. Of course, some of the talk had reached the ears of that mother's children. Somehow the speakers and musicians had struggled their way through the memorial with thoughts and melodies. The religious leader preached his awkward sermon. Time had passed and no one's heart had changed. Then as the musicians put their instruments away, suddenly everything changed. A daughter about ten years old left her place beside her father in the front of the chapel and walked up the few steps to the pulpit—unscheduled, unannounced. Maybe she had some doubts of her own. Surely she'd had her struggles in a home where trauma was deep enough to bring such a tragic end to a life. Yet this little girl taught the lesson of the day when she said, "I loved my mother. Please talk nice about her. She was great to me, and she smelled good every morning."

Many of us went home humbled, diligently resolving to "smell good every morning." It was the least we women could do, and it might make all the difference.

A great civic and Church leader whose influence has been felt worldwide credits his widowed mother for shaping his beginnings. He writes:

> A daughter and I were recently discussing her return home at an hour that seemed questionable to me. I shared with her an experience with my wonderful mother. I had spent some years away at schools and missions and wars, and the two of us were now alone at home. I returned from an appointment one evening at midnight to find the light still on in Mother's little bedroom. As I had always done, I reported in to Mom, sat on her bed, and kidded with her a little. I asked her why she was still awake. "I am waiting for you," she said.
>
> I said, "Did you wait for me while I was on a mission, Mom, or at sea, or in battle?"
>
> Her answer was calm and sweet. She gave me that little pat on the knee that reflects the mature compassion of the wise for the ignorant, and said: "No, that would have been foolish. I just knelt down here by my bed and talked to the Lord about my boy. I told him what kind of man I believed you to be and wanted you to be, and prayed for his watchful care of you, and then left you in his hands and went to sleep. But now you are home," she said, "and you can count on it that I will be interested in you as long as I live." (Marion D. Hanks, *The Gift of Self* [Salt Lake City: Bookcraft, 1974], pp. 289–90.)

A friend of mine had enjoyed a rich and lengthy life with a husband who loved her and whom she adored. They had reared a fine family. Together they had buried precious loved ones and adopted a child from another race who needed a home. They had coped with financial disaster, awesome professional responsibility, some serious disappointments, and finally with sweet public success.

Then he died suddenly in his sleep. Out of the details of their life, such closeness had developed that when death claimed the husband, the wife felt the sun would never shine again. She wondered that people walked the city streets, smiling. She realized at last that her grief was overly long and ultimately useless, but she could not bring it to an end.

She responded to an opportunity to be a volunteer in a local pediatric hospital. Her job was to register the children being brought there for medical help. All day long she dealt with people suffering from problems, but she was oblivious to them because she still wallowed in her own grief.

One day a mother came in with a baby so deformed and pitifully stricken that my friend was startled out of her self-centered blindness. The baby's mother cheerfully reached into the heart of the grieving widow in a way that swept away bitterness and all feelings of personal uselessness. The baby's mother was a "blessing-counting" individual. She explained to the widow that she felt especially honored to be given this particularly troubled baby, this unfortunate bit of humanity, to care for. "God gave this baby to me because he knew I'd love him well. Isn't that an honor for me?" This wonderful mother taught another mother the lesson of gratitude and confidence before God.

To Mother

From the children:
Touch me soft
Be gentle
Listen to me
Care
Let me see
Your eyes
So I will know
You're there.

From their father:
Touch me, love,
Be tender
Let me speak my
Part.
Bathe me
With your eyes, dear,
That I may know
Your heart.

From Heavenly Father:
Reach me now.
Be prayerful.
Let your spirit shine.
Seek me—
For the answers
To fill your heart
Are mine!

—Elaine Cannon

Mother Eve

And Adam called his wife's name Eve; because she was
the mother of all living.

—Genesis 3:20

We are indebted to Robert Frost for this delightful insight into
Mother Eve:

Never Again Would Birds' Song Be the Same

He would declare and could himself believe
That the birds there in all the garden round
From having heard the daylong voice of Eve
Had added to their own an oversound,
Her tone of meaning but without the words.
Admittedly an eloquence so soft
Could only have had an influence on birds
When call or laughter carried it aloft.
Be that as may be, she was in their song.
Moreover her voice upon their voices crossed
Had now persisted in the woods so long
That probably it never would be lost.
Never again would birds' song be the same.
And to do that to birds was why she came.
(*The Poetry of Robert Frost,* ed. Edward Connery
Lathem [New York: Holt, Rinehart and Winston, 1969],
pp. 338–39.)

Mother Eve was there in the first place, stirring Adam into a higher way of living by descending into hardship. In this way Eve brought about Motherhood. God's plan is for all of his children to have opportunities to grow, to know love, and to become more Christlike. What better way than family life to experience these things? Eve started us on the path as the mother of all living.

President Joseph Fielding Smith paid Eve a wonderful tribute during a general conference address when he said that he looked forward to meeting Mother Eve because she was so courageous and insightful. Suddenly a murmur passed through the congregation. Eve wasn't just a beautiful, naughty girl! She was not a mindless innocent. She was a woman of understanding—intuitively wise, a woman longing to reach her fullest potential and anxious to risk all as a helpmeet to her Adam.

She was aware of the consequences of their choice and explained the situation to Adam. He might have been content to loll about the garden in complacent comfort endlessly, if it hadn't been for Eve. They needed a world to grow in. Adam needed a work to do—to toil and reap by the sweat of his brow, to fail and repeat the effort, growing in strength and stature in the process. Together—as all men and women must do—Adam and Eve learned the meaning of life, to know good from evil, right from wrong, and the sweetness of pleasure after pain.

Eve might have felt that Adam wasn't cast out of the Garden of Eden in punishment so much as he was liberated from it, because Adam was no longer relaxed, pampered, childlike. Louis Untermeyer poetically suggested that Eve might even have been proud of what she did; although God had created a creature out of the dust, she had helped him become a man.

And Eve? She became his prize, his wife, his companion, his compensation and source of peace, his center of passion. She was all that any man wants in a woman and mother, and her echo has carried through women since this beginning of time.

As he traveled around the world, President Spencer W. Kimball often reminded the sisters that there can be no heaven without righteous women. And there isn't much heaven on earth without such women either! Women follow in the footsteps of Eve and down the generations have had a mighty adventure doing it. Not all women have known ease, honor and credit, fulfillment in love, grand opportunities for skill training and meaningful application of knowledge, or even a place in history. But women have made all the difference to men who have. Without the nurturing and guiding of mothers, there would never have been a Michelangelo, a Bach, a Cicero, an Isaac or a Jacob, a Goethe or a Robert Frost, a Winston Churchill or a Joseph Smith.

To be an Eve in any time period was exciting, but now is the day for true excitement as women figure prominently in the winding-up scenes before Christ comes to bring peace on earth. The last days are prophesied to be the most trying, the most wicked, the most wretched, the most shocking, the most destructive and heart wrenching ever to trouble people. Mother Eve met her challenges with Cain and Abel and set a pattern of involvement and succor in the lives of others. Today a righteous woman's strength and influence are the most golden of opportunities to influence children—and what children! They are representatives of the royal generation saved to come forth in the latter days to make ready a covenant people to receive Jesus Christ.

Eve began as the mother of mankind. She remains the ultimate mover of men. Eve started it all, but a choice group of women will help in the wrapping up. You, Mother, are a very reasonable facsimile of Eve!

Mother in Heaven

You [women] are daughters of God. You are precious.
You are made in the image of our heavenly Mother.
—Spencer W. Kimball

Wwhat an exciting image to plant in a woman's mind! A Mother in Heaven? Wonderful! Sometimes a mother needs a Mother!

A hardworking, self-sacrificing woman can find herself longing for a nurturer, a champion, a cheerleader, a hug of hope, someone like a Heavenly Mother. It can be comforting for women to think about a Mother in Heaven. Doing so doesn't diminish the grandeur of God the Heavenly Father, but rather simply reveals a childlike longing for Someone—a Heavenly Mother—that comes from a deep well inside the heart.

Today's woman is searching for her deepest identity. The world's rapid changes have opened not only doors long closed to women in the marketplace and professional arenas but also the blinds to their position in theology.

Does God really care about women? Why aren't women mentioned more in scripture? Do women have to fight for their place before God as in any male-dominated setting (home included!)? If there is a God in heaven, if we are all children of God, then isn't there a Goddess, a mother God?

Hoping against hope, the searching woman longs for a positive answer. It just seems right! However, sure information on the subject of a Mother in Heaven is scant.

Women of many organized religions are searching after an understanding of female deity. They yearn after real equality—equality not legislated or bestowed as a token. As part of the search, some have insisted on being admitted to clergy positions. Some have engaged in the mental struggle of getting answers about their spiritual origin in the hope of bolstering their understanding.

Scholars in ancient religious studies have found some evidence of teachings about a divine mother and about deity with female attributes. Why is so little said in later texts? In the early seasons of organized religion, somewhere in the first century following the mission and subsequent crucifixion of Christ, female deity began to be omitted from the collections of dogma of the Christian church. Men were gathering commandments, parables, and sacred history, giving women little place. However, in the thirteenth verse of the last chapter of Isaiah is an interesting comfort that mothers—women—should remember: "As one whom his mother comforteth, so will I comfort you."

The nicest kind of imagery!

Part of the restoration of the gospel of Jesus Christ is the renewed knowledge of the plan of life and of a Mother in Heaven. Even though the idea of a Mother in Heaven has not been central in expounded Church doctrine, we clearly understand that in heaven parents are *not* single and that in order to reach the most glorious eternal place, man and woman must follow the same covenant path together. Though the scriptures contain only hints of the nature of a Mother in Heaven, statements by Church Presidents and other prophetic teachers support such a doctrine. (Remember that a belief in a Mother in Heaven who is a partner with God in creation and procreation is not the same as the heavy emphasis on Mariology in the Roman Catholic tradition.)

Elohim, the name-title for God, suggests the plural form of the Caananite *El* or the Hebrew *Eloah*. It is used in various Hebrew combinations to describe the highest God. It is the majestic title of the ultimate Deity. The text of Genesis 1:27, "So God created man in his own image, in the image of God created he him; *male and female* created he them" (emphasis added), may be read to mean that "God" is plural.

For faithful Latter-day Saints, the concept of an eternal family is more than a firm belief—it governs our way of life. It is the eternal plan of life, stretching from premortality through eternity. We believe that parenthood requires both a father and a mother, whether for the creation of spirits in the premortal life or of the physical tabernacles on earth. A Heavenly Mother shares parenthood with the Heavenly Father. This concept implies that our beloved Heavenly Mother is like our Father in glory, perfection, compassion, wisdom, and holiness. (See Elaine Anderson Cannon, "Mother in Heaven," in *Encyclopedia of Mormonism*, ed. Daniel H. Ludlow, 5 vols. [New York: Macmillan, 1992], 2:961.)

Yes, we have a Mother in Heaven, and, with all appropriate honor, we say that we should consider trying to be like her!

Now, just for the comfort of it, read again the last two verses taken from the familiar hymn by Eliza R. Snow, "O My Father":

> I had learned to call thee Father,
> Thru thy Spirit from on high,
> But, until the key of knowledge
> Was restored, I knew not why.
> In the heav'ns are parents single?
> No, the thought makes reason stare!
> Truth is reason; truth eternal
> Tells me I've a mother there.

> When I leave this frail existence,
> When I lay this mortal by,
> Father, Mother, may I meet you
> In your royal courts on high?
> Then, at length, when I've completed
> All you sent me forth to do,
> With your mutual approbation
> Let me come and dwell with you.
> (*Hymns,* no. 292.)

Mother: Birth and Death

Robert Browning wrote, "Womanliness means only motherhood; all love begins and ends there." So does birth and usually death.

When our daughter-in-law was in the last heartbreaking moments of life, she called her own mother and me to her bedside. No one else was in the room. She said, "Mother, I want to tell you something in front of Elaine. I want you to love Jamie's new wife as you love me so that we can be all one happy family." It was a heart crusher. We had to face the truth that she knew the truth about her future. The courage it took for her to speak of such a thing revealed her noble character and set the pattern for family behavior ever after. It has been easy—not awkward—to envelop each other in love. The new mother who ultimately came into the home with a child of her own was like a daughter to the family who had lost their own only daughter to an untimely death.

Every mother who has been through childbearing understands the trip through the "valley of the shadow of death." Women who play mothering roles of all kinds often risk their lives for their inherited offspring. I think of the lovely friend who nursed an adopted son through agonizing months as he gradually, painfully died of AIDS. This was in a time when the full understanding of the disease wasn't known nor the necessary treatment and precautions for dealing with this ravaging problem. I think of the mother who was a surrogate mother for her daughter who medically could not have children of her own. I think of an older mother who gave a kidney for her son and nearly lost her own life to save his—they both lost.

Our fourth child was born close to Christmas. I had fallen down a flight of stairs and been rushed to the hospital, where I was delivered of this fine child without the help of anesthetic. I felt ashamed the whole time, thinking of pioneer women suffering childbirth on the floor of a covered wagon! But this is an important point because I was very alert instead of groggy when they brought my baby to me for the first feeding.

Here she was only a good-sized lump before, and seconds later a new life in the history of womankind. However, as I snuggled her to me, a strange feeling came over me. This bundle wasn't mine! I had scarcely seen her at the time of the birth, so I couldn't base the feeling on her appearance. Deep inside me a faint stirring began that there had been a mistake. I tried to discount the idea and went back to the nursing, only to have the feeling well up within me again. It was stronger this time, so I checked the name tag against my own bracelet tag. They matched. Then I undressed the infant—a girl. Okay. I knew I'd had a girl. But my heart started to thump then: it just wasn't *my* girl. I love all of Heavenly Father's children, but if I had a choice, of course I wanted to nurture the child that had formed in my womb.

Again I took up the task of encouraging the infant to breastfeed. But I was restless and frustrated. I quickly checked the name written in tape across the baby's back, as was the practice at birth in those days. *Cannon.* The name tallied with mine, and the room number was correct.

I told myself to settle down. I asked myself, "What more do you want, Elaine?"

My own baby!

The more I tried putting it out of my mind, blaming Christmas hysteria, the more sure I was that this child, though darling, belonged to somebody else.

And somebody else had my baby.

So with heart throbbing and my ears buzzing, I rang the nurse and told her my problem. She went through the checking-it-out ritual I had followed. She insisted that I was just groggy, too fresh from the delivery room.

"But I'm not groggy. I had no anesthetic. I just *know* she isn't mine!" I lamely explained.

The more she tried to silence me, the harder my heart pounded, assuring me that I was right and she was wrong.

She lost her patience and her nurse's required cool. She went for the head nurse, and we went all through it again. This lady, however, was deeply annoyed with me and swept that baby out of my arms and out of the room.

Such loneliness swept over me! I started to cry and to pray hard. I knew I had been prompted by the Holy Ghost about the mistake, but I didn't know how to rectify the wrong. Suddenly an idea occurred to me to call the hospital administrator. It was evening and he was at home for dinner, but when he heard my story he came at once and initiated an investigation. He was a fine member of the Church and understood my story about promptings of the Spirit.

Fortunately, at that time a baby's footprints were taken in the delivery room while the infant was still connected to the mother. When the comparisons were made, it was proven that the baby I had been given wasn't mine. The *Cannon* tape had been inadvertently put on the back of the wrong one of two babies born at the same time during the sacred season of celebrating.

When at last I was brought my own baby, the Spirit confirmed to me that this was truly my child. She grew up with her father's unmistakable physical features.

She died as a young mother. In the last stages of her illness, we spent long hours by her bedside. She would tell me stories about her children, and I would tell her stories about her life. One day, despite feeling especially blue, she mustered up her wonderful humor and teasingly asked me if it were possible if again she could have been mixed up with somebody else and given the wrong terminal illness.

Mary F. Foulger wrote of an idea that many mothers can relate to:

> Our six children were young and completely dependent when my husband invited me to accompany him on a business trip. I had never before been far away from my nest of little

ones. At first I was delighted, but as my departure drew near I became obsessed with fear. If something happened to me, what would become of them? I worked myself into such a frenzy that the night before I was to leave I spent the night composing a letter of instruction to one I prayed would care for them in case I didn't return. I listed all the things I felt were essential to their welfare, and then added a PS: "Please put your arms around them often."

If not my arms, then her arms—for a mother's arms encircle a child with tender restraint, security, love. They protect against fear, harm, and evil. . . .

For those who have not yet borne a child—exercise motherhood. Let your arms be an extension of the Savior's in providing love and security for all his children. . . .

My mother died three weeks before my first child was born. How I longed for her. . . . I have felt the Lord's arms encircled about me through sacred sisterhood, through enlightenment and training received in Relief Society. ("Motherhood and the Family," *Ensign*, November 1980, p. 105.)

Eudora Welty, a noted author of whom I am very fond, wrote a charming piece about birth and death in which she laughingly lamented that she doubted whether any child she ever knew was told any more than she was about how babies came about. In fact, Eudora doubted that her own grandmother ever told her own mother (when she was a child) any more than she had told Eudora. She wrote:

In my mother's bottom bureau drawer in her bedroom she kept treasures of hers in boxes. . . . One day I noticed . . . a small white cardboard box such as her engraved calling cards came in from the printing house. It was tightly closed, but I opened it, to find to my puzzlement and covetousness two polished buffalo nickels, embedded in white cotton. I rushed with this opened box to my mother and asked if I could run out and spend the nickels.

"No!" she exclaimed in a most passionate way. She seized the box into her own hands. I begged her; somehow I had started to cry. Then she sat down, drew me to her, and told me that I had had a little brother who had come before I did, and who had died as a baby before I was born. And these two nickels that I'd wanted to claim as my find were his. They had lain on his eyelids, for a purpose untold and unimaginable.

Eudora's mother explained that when it came to a choice in saving her life or the baby boy's the father had chosen to have the doctors save his wife. But they had never told Eudora about having an older brother. She wrote, "She'd told me the wrong secret—not how babies could come but how they could die, how they could be forgotten about." (*One Writer's Beginnings* [Cambridge, Massachusetts: Harvard University Press, 1984], pp. 16–17.)

The phrase "Good night, my darling" seems the perfect farewell to a loved one slipping into the body's final rest. Eleanor Farjeon said that one of the cadences that lingers forever in her ears is the tone of her mother's voice as she tucked her in bed as a child. Then when the tables were turned and Eleanor was keeping watch on her dying mother, the mother said again, "Good night, my darling." The tone and the smile were like reassurance to a child, only this time Eleanor felt her mother's comfort and direction implying, "Don't think of me in pain, don't think of anything tonight but that you are my darling—and sleep well."

Eleanor finished the story: "The Sunday before she died, when she had been so ill and was so tired that life scarcely flickered in her, I sat holding her hand, now and then whispering something into the silence that was falling between us. 'You've been the sweetest mother to us.' She turned her head, and opened her heavy lids, and her eyes were quite dark in her white, gentle face. The smile came: 'I've had the sweetest children.' And when I kissed her, before leaving her, suddenly the exquisite girlish voice, sweet, almost happy—'Good night, my darling.'"

Mothering women brush death frequently through life—their own or someone's they love. This kind of experience, lived through, demands resolution. There is something of being born again when one is getting ready for death. Whether death comes or is merely postponed seems unimportant, for the strings have been juggled and the lessons learned . . . *as if!*

Florida Scott-Maxwell before her death wrote: "It has taken me all the time I've had to become myself, yet now that I am old there are times when I feel I am barely here, no room for me at all. I remember that in the last months of my pregnancies the child seemed to claim almost all my body, my strength, my breath, and I held on wondering if my burden was my enemy, uncertain as to whether my life was at all mine. Is life a pregnancy? That would make death a birth." (*The Measure of My Days* [New York: Alfred A. Knopf, 1968], p. 76.)

There is healing when one believes, as I believe, that there are more glorious days and comforts enough in a heavenly new environment beyond this one. Death is then a birth.

Mother and Other Mothers

But we were gentle among you, even as a nurse
cherisheth her children: so being affectionately desirous
of you, we were willing to have imparted unto you, not
the gospel of God only, but also our own souls, because
ye were dear unto us.

— 1 Thessalonians 2:7–8

One Mother's Day, the children in the church meeting were distributing flowers to their mothers, who were standing on invitation for their annual moment of glory! Our little grandson eagerly took a quivering pink begonia in a gold-foil pot and started purposefully down the aisle. Suddenly he stopped and turned back. His mother, he remembered, was not there. She had passed away some weeks before. Later he sadly said to me, "I didn't know mothers were so important. I didn't have anyone to give the flower to."

The following Thanksgiving the family was counting their blessings around the table following the feast. There was a new mother in the home now with heart enough to deal with the trauma of change. The smallest child took his turn. "I am thankful for my other mother," he said shyly. "Me, too!" echoed the brother who had turned his begonia plant back in on Mother's Day.

The *other mother.* The phrase has hung in my heart since then, and over the years I've noticed many women make a difference playing the part of the other mother.

Mother is more than a title, a happenstance of nature, an assignment because there are children in a home. Acts of love have been done by women in many situations—angels for a day, season, or lifetime in the holy business of nurturing and warming . . . of mothering.

The *American Heritage* dictionary defines *mother:* "a female parent; a female who holds a position of authority or responsibility similar to a mother; to give birth to, . . . to create; produce . . . or, to watch over, nourish, and protect."

Sounds impressive—and accurate—whether describing the birth mother or the adoptive parent, the blood relative or the kind soul who takes on the role of influence and unequivocal caring of a child.

In his October 1992 general conference address, Elder Glenn L. Pace gave a personal perspective to an other mother in his life who, for a season, was very important to him:

> When I was young I was overly dependent on my older sister. For example, I was a fussy eater, and when we went to visit our grandparents I was constantly faced with being offered food I didn't like. To minimize my embarrassment, when the plate was passed to me, I would turn to my sister and ask, "Collene, do I like this?"
>
> If it was familiar and she knew I didn't like it, she would say, "No, he doesn't like that."
>
> I could then say to Grandma, "She's right, I don't like it."
>
> If it was something we hadn't eaten before she would say, "Just a minute," and taste it, and then tell me if I liked it or not. If she said I didn't like it, no amount of coaxing could get me to eat it. ("Spiritual Revival," *Ensign,* November 1992, p. 11.)

We knew a family who had moved along through life on star-spangled wings. There were seven little children all in a tight row, two houses, plentiful holdings, and a place in choice social circles. They were deeply devoted to one another, and as proof of their goal for closeness, mother, father, and every child had a first name that began with the letter *M.* Then, following the birth of a new baby, the mother suddenly, and cruelly it seemed, died.

After a while the father married again. His new wife was young, sophisticated, and successful in glamorous work. She had no children of her own. And her first name did not begin with *M.*

People wondered and worried. But she became an energetic friend and counselor to the growing family. One by one the children were carefully guided through peer pressure and homework, and prepared for missions and temple marriage. She added something of herself to their growth, and their lives opened up beyond themselves. She became an other mother, and with the endearing title she earned, her name began with *M* after all!

I think often of the powerful lesson I learned (and have shared now countless times) from a wine salesman with Italian roots who told me his story while we were airplane-seat companions. He was the youngest of five little children when their mother died. The father was a highly successful wine merchant in the United States. He promptly went back to Italy to find a proper mother for his brood. He fell in love with a schoolteacher, brought her back to the United States, settled her comfortably in the family home, and went on about his demanding business of production and travel. She had two children of her own, and the years passed. At an elaborate celebration for the twenty-fifth wedding anniversary, my traveling companion learned a powerful secret. He said, "I was sitting with our rebellious teenagers and wondering how we were going to survive these years. I looked over at that remarkable woman who had become mother to me when I was a toddler. I wondered how she did what she did. How did she make us all feel loved until we knew no difference between her own children and the rest of us from a different mother? She loved us and I loved her! I got up and went over to her to tell her so. Then I asked her how she did it—how did she make us all feel so blessedly loved?"

"What did she say?" I quickly asked, my head reeling with remembrance of numerous households struggling with similar problems.

He continued, "She said to me, 'Oh, son, I loved your father and so I loved his children.' That's the secret!"

He was weeping now as he told me. My own heart leapt to understand that this was the secret of life: we love the Father and then we will love his children.

Sometimes a mother needs a mother of her own when the ability to keep giving is stifled by depression, fatigue, or illness. I once had to shut myself and our four little ones under six into the nursery. I had a fever of 104 degrees, and I was pregnant again. Staying upright was no longer a viable option. In my misery I curled up on a youth bed to keep a watchful eye on our precious destroying angels. Balls and baby bottles sailed over my head while dark thoughts stirred my mind. My young husband was a conscientious new bishop who was always visiting the sick, and I wondered how sick one had to be to get the bishop to come and call in our home!

I didn't feel like much of a mother—more like a big baby, such was my self-pity.

Then the doorbell rang, and I dragged from the bed to peer through the window to the front porch. There stood the Relief Society president, an older woman who worked closely with my young husband in the welfare needs of our ward. She was old enough to be my mother, and I was appalled that she should catch me in my failure, in this house of chaos where no mother's hand had been raised recently to do more than keep the little ones from hurting each other.

The stampede to answer the doorbell came from children aching for release from the confinement of the nursery. While I called through the window that I was ill and would see her another time, the children were already opening the door for her.

Then the most marvelous bit of "other mothering" occurred. This time I was the child being taught lifesaving lessons. This fine friend explained that she had been driving by our house and had felt prompted by the Spirit that help was needed therein.

Lesson one: Be in tune and respond to the promptings of the Spirit.

She had hurried home to get her ever-ready Friendship Bag, full of supplies and surprises for the sick and afflicted.

Lesson two: Be prepared and equipped to meet the need.

Returning to our home, she rang the doorbell until there was a response.

Lesson three: Don't give up too soon in doing your good deeds!

She told me to lie down on the living room couch while she lured the children to the kitchen table with cookies and new coloring books. She would help me in a moment. In relief, I obeyed.

Lesson four: Even a mother needs a mother on occasion.

Sister Jensen took my foot in her hands, ignoring my protests of embarrassment that she would be doing that to *me!* She talked quietly and comfortingly, all the while massaging each foot while she healed my soul. There was quiet for a moment, and then I got lesson five: "Love your partner, Elaine. Love him enough so that he has plenty to give his ward members. Let your bishop-husband be a good shepherd."

Belle S. Spafford spent a lifetime mothering mothers and teaching women to be womanly in all the ways important to Heavenly Father and his children on earth. She was an impressive example, too, as general president of the Relief Society. At the end of her life she herself needed close personal attention, so she was moved into the home of a granddaughter, who became, for a time, a kind of other mother to her grandmother.

Sister Spafford insisted on having a hospital bed in the room. It was absolutely necessary, she explained, because the side rails could be used as a ladder for the little girl in the family to climb up for visits with Great-grandmother. Each day until the last, Sister Spafford and the small child snuggled on a single pillow, the little one wrapped in the arms of that grande dame—encircled in the arms of her love. After observing all her teaching and all the excellent examples, I choose to remember Sister Spafford in this simple scene reminiscent of the Savior's promise, "Be faithful and diligent in keeping the commandments of God, and I will encircle thee in the arms of my love" (D&C 6:20).

In the special sisterhood of overworked mothers, the best blessing and most effusive praise surely must go to the good women who are willing to love, reassure, and reinforce somebody else's child.

What about the role of adoptive mother?

What joy an adopted baby brings to the aching arms of the barren woman who then becomes its mother!

We hear countless tender expressions from families who have adopted children. Often such families feel an assurance that a particular spirit child of Heavenly Father belongs in a certain family even if his birth channel was not there.

Over the years I have responded in friendship to young women who have been tried in this manner. I remember with acute tenderness one beautiful sixteen-year-old unwed mother who came to me for help. She had been wisely counseled that two wrongs don't make a right, and so she had given up her baby for adoption. But she was miserable. She had grieved over her decision for six months. She was confused because her arms, she said, kept aching like the itch an amputee feels in the toe of his long-gone foot.

We took this young woman to visit a lady with a newly adopted baby. This was a home with the distinct advantages of stability and security, where parenthood had been urgently desired and agonizingly delayed. In that most beautiful rite among women, our hostess cuddled to her own breast this precious infant who had come forth from another's womb. She spoke glowingly of the unknown mother.

"I know that she must have wanted to keep this baby—he is so beautiful. But, of course, she gave him up so he could have a real home, a better chance at life than she herself could provide at this time. So I'll mother this little spirit child of our Heavenly Father, and I'll care for the body that the unselfish, unknown girl provided. I'll mother this little boy with all of me, grateful for joy I might not have known. We prayed earnestly for a baby because we had not been able to have one of our own. We feel this boy is an answer to our prayer, that he belongs in our home."

It was a new perspective of motherhood for the troubled sixteen-year-old. Peace came with the awareness that it was all right to have another be mother to the baby she had borne.

And what of the other mother—the one who because of unfortunate happenings gives up her baby for adoption?

Recently I received a letter from a woman who had given a baby up for adoption years ago. She gave me permission to share parts of a letter that she wrote to the daughter she had given up.

Dear Kim:

The most wonderful thing happened to me today. I received a very special phone call. It was from your mother. What a surprise and what a wonderful person she is. She told me many interesting things about you—how pretty you are and sweet and kind; how your brothers and sisters look up to you. Thank you for being that kind of girl.

I truly hope that I may say some things in this letter that will be of comfort to you. I was given the unique experience of bringing you into this life. I never did see you, but I knew you were a choice spirit all the time I was carrying you within me.

At the time I became pregnant with you, I was not married. I fell deeply in love with a man and became pregnant. I wanted to get married *very much*, but he decided to marry somebody else.

At this time, I had been divorced from my first husband for three years. I had two little girls who had missed having their daddy because he never came to see them. Sometimes people are very selfish and they can only think of themselves. That is how their father was, and I saw the pain it caused. I wanted a better life for you. I wanted you to have both a loving mom and dad. I wanted your parents to be married in the temple. I wanted you to be sealed to them. That's how much I loved *you!*

Some people seem to think a mother doesn't love her child when she decides to have the child adopted. But I feel that most mothers who really care and who really love the child have the child adopted because they *love* that child more than themselves!

I loved you, all through my pregnancy, and I loved you when you were born. I love you still today. I didn't see you at birth because I knew that if I did, I wouldn't be able to let you go. My parents—your grandparents—did get to see you. Your grandmother wanted to make sure you were all right. And she told me you were. She told me you were a beautiful girl, just as your mother told me today. Your parents must love you a great deal to allow themselves to contact me.

At first, the heartache of not being able to see you and hold you in my arms and to rear you was unbearable. As the years have gone on, I have tried to think of your happiness with your family now, and I have prayed for strength, and I know Heavenly Father has given me comfort for doing the right thing for you.

Remember the story in the Bible of the two women who fought over their child? And King Solomon told the women that if they were going to fight he would cut the baby in half, and give each a half! Then the real mother stood up and told the king to give the baby to the other woman rather than destroy it. King Solomon knew who the real mother was then.

Another story from the Bible tells of a Hebrew woman who put her baby in a basket among the reeds by a riverbank to save him from being killed along with other infants. And that baby was raised in a royal family and grew up to become Moses!

Even in biblical times, there were mothers who felt it was

better for someone else to raise and care for their children. But the mother never stopped loving them or missing them. In the two stories I've mentioned, both of these mothers wanted their children spared from pain and sorrow. They wanted a better life for their child than they could have with them at this time. They wanted this enough to give them away.

Someday, when Heavenly Father wants and the time is right, we will meet in person. Thank you for your life and for caring about me.

When I made my first pilgrimage to Golgotha I was a young mother. I was caught up in the joy of having children belong to me. I had had a baby born at Christmas, and I wondered how Mary could have given Jesus up. There at the place of the crucifixion of her Son, I wondered where Mary had stood. Surely it was sacred ground—Jesus loved his mother:

> Now there stood by the cross of Jesus his mother. . . .
> When Jesus therefore saw his mother, and the disciple standing by, whom he loved, he saith unto this mother, Woman, behold thy son!
> Then saith he to the disciple, Behold thy mother! And from that hour that disciple took her unto his own home. (John 19:25–27.)

Even Mary was an other mother.

Years ago I came across a quaint but compelling poem by Lydia B. Alder published in an early issue of the *Instructor* magazine. It was titled "Two Mothers." These following lines are excerpted from that piece:

> I am a-weary weeping so,
> My heart throbs with its pain,
> I close my eyes to ease my woe,
> And see it all again.
> My slain—the Crucified—my Son,
> There hanging on the tree!
> 'Twas not for wrong that he had done—
> E'en then he thought of me.
> That other mother, coming near—

Within her eyes there burns
A quenchless fire—a with'ring fear,
That ev'ry solace spurns.
I pity her—have anger none,
But O, so much of joy,
For love divine gave me a Son—
A Judas was her boy.
"O pity, Mary, hear me, hear!"
Prone on the earth she lies,
For grief so deep there is no tear
To lave the burning eyes.
But Mother Mary lifts her up,
And soothes her with caress,
Adds sweetness to her bitter cup,
And makes her own pain less.

Surely these lines give guidance to all who are mothers, whether by an act of nature, by choice, or by circumstance. We are, after all, agents for Heavenly Father, his angels for a season in helping to bring some peace and joy to others and in preparing a child to go forth. Mothers and other mothers who are good at loving make all the difference.

Mother: An Example of the Believer

Be thou an example of the believers, in word, in
conversation, in charity, in spirit, in faith, in purity.
—1 Timothy 4:12

When one of our children was very young but well endowed
with a keen mind, he said something that, given my limitations, set
me thinking.

He said, "I'd certainly hate to be a parent or a teacher."

"Oh?" I said, gamely scrubbing the floor one more time.
"Why is that?"

Immediately I began berating myself because I wasn't more
alert—or something! Kids—why did I let them do this to me?
"Why?" I asked him again. "Why would you hate to be a parent or
a teacher?"

"Well, it's too hard."

The boy was perceptive, I thought happily. But what had I
done to turn him off to being a parent? I persisted, "Surely you
want to have children of your own someday!" I finished lamely,
"That means you'll have to be a kind of teacher, too."

"Yeah, well, it's too hard, I think. They have to be believable."

"Right!" I exclaimed, struggling to get up and then walking
swiftly toward my scriptures.

I read to him what Paul wrote to Timothy: "Let no man de-
spise thy youth: but be thou an example of the believers, in word,
in conversation, in charity, in spirit, in faith, in purity. . . . Neglect

not the gift that is in thee, which was given thee by prophecy, with the laying on of . . . hands." (1 Timothy 4:12, 14.)

I emphasized the part about "be thou an example of the believers." Isn't that what any mother should teach her children? Regardless of what any teacher or leader or parent seems to be, the children themselves have the responsibility (and the privilege) to choose to believe and behave as examples of believers in the gospel of Jesus Christ. If we do not teach them anything else, we need to teach them that.

Children have agency to act and think on their own, but we must help them learn correct principles before they try to govern themselves. A believing mother is more likely to rear up a believing child. A believing child is apt to cope with all the shifting prisms of life.

Jesus knows what is best for us and our children. He has clearly told us what we should teach them by example and precept. When he was on the American continent, he warned of false prophets and promised salvation to those who do the Father's will. He also said, "If ye then, being evil, know how to give good gifts unto your children, how much more shall your Father who is in heaven give good things to them that ask him? Therefore, all things whatsoever ye would that men should do to you, do ye even so to them." (3 Nephi 14:11–12.)

Since a mother meets a child's first beginnings, since his quickest learnings and the stimulation of his responses are formed while he is very young, since Satan is bound against tempting an innocent child before the age of eight, the early years are golden. A mother's influence is at its peak. Young women will do well to prepare themselves before the mothering begins.

Carol Lynn Pearson wrote these elegant lines on preparing to be part of God's mothering plan for his spirit children on earth:

On Nest Building

Mud is not bad for nest building.
Mud and sticks
And a fallen feather or two will do
And require no reaching.
I could rest there, with my tiny ones,
Sound for the season, at least.

> But—
> If I may fly awhile—
> If I may cut through a sunset going out
> And a rainbow coming back,
> Color upon color sealed in my eyes—
> If I may have the unboundaried skies
> For my study,
> Clouds, cities, rivers for my rooms—
> If I may search the centuries
> For melody and meaning—
> If I may try for the sun—
>
> I shall come back
> Bearing such beauties
> Gleaned from God's and man's very best.
> I shall come filled.
>
> And then—
> Oh, the nest that I can build!
> (*The Flight and the Nest* [Salt Lake City:
> Bookcraft, 1975], p. v.)

Prepare to build your own nest and you'll be believable!

Mothers, please ensure that your own example is one of faith, of obedience to God's commandments, of positive support of General Authorities and other Church leaders, and of devotion to scripture study. Keep consistent and clear standards for every Sabbath's activities and for Church attendance. Positive traditions that a mother can build with her children include celebrating Christ-centered Christmases, serving neighbors, supporting community events, having the full-time missionaries to dinner, and listening to general conference. Honesty, patience, giving, loving, and helping—all begin in the home.

Children are so quick to pick up on a dichotomy, like the little girl who said, "Mommy, why do we have to go to church?"

And the mommy replied, "To learn the doctrine of the kingdom."

The little girl said, "Don't we already *know* more than we *do?*"

In the October 1986 general conference, Elder Boyd K. Packer said that studying gospel doctrine "will improve behavior quicker than a study of behavior will improve behavior. Preoccupation with unworthy behavior can lead to unworthy behavior." ("Little Children," *Ensign,* November 1986, p. 17.)

The scriptures and Church history provide excellent precedents for mothers who want to be examples of the believers. Consider the sons of Helaman, the fine stripling (or youthful) sons who never had fought, yet they didn't fear death; they thought more of the liberty of their fathers than they did of their own lives. How well they had been taught by their mothers! They did not doubt that God would deliver them if they went to war. They told this to Helaman and said, "We do not doubt our mothers knew it." (See Alma 56:45–48.)

They went into battle guarded by the faith of their mothers' faith in God. This faith in their mothers' faith brought forth faith in themselves to do what was right. Their first real test was a remarkable battle that took great courage and cunning to drive back the enemy. When it was over, Helaman went to look for his two thousand, afraid that he would find many slain. But "behold, to my great joy, there had not one soul of them fallen to the earth; yea, and they had fought as if with the strength of God; yea, never were men known to have fought with such miraculous strength" (Alma 56:56). They fought this way until the enemy became frightened and delivered themselves. After further battles without losing a single life, Helaman recounted the skill and courage of these young warriors. In describing them, he wrote of their exceeding faith: "We do justly ascribe it to the miraculous power of God, because of their exceeding faith in that which they had been taught to believe—that there was a just God, and whosoever did not doubt, that they should be preserved by his marvelous power" (Alma 57:26). Helaman also wrote, "And I did remember the words which they said unto me that their mothers had taught them. . . . It was these my sons . . . to whom we owe this great victory; for it was they who did beat the Lamanites." (Alma 57: 21–22.)

Speaking of faith, Paul reminded Timothy that his heritage of faith came from his grandmother and mother: "I call to remembrance the unfeigned faith that is in thee, which dwelt first in thy grandmother Lois, and thy mother Eunice; and I am persuaded that in thee also" (2 Timothy 1:5). Paul also urged the Saints to follow after the things which "make for peace, and things wherewith one may edify another" (Romans 14:19).

Oh, it does help to have mentors, muses, friends, and teachers of one kind or another, who not only know and share eternal truths but also are themselves examples, living proofs of the value in God's plan, women who stand firm in the faith.

God has always upheld his faithful daughters. Sister Amanda Smith suffered through the ill-fated Haun's Mill massacre, in which she lost her husband and a little son to barbarian mobsters who brutally butchered them. After Alma, another of her sons, had his hip shot away in gleeful sport by the inhuman torturers, his mother carried him to their tent, knowing that no physician was available and praying desperately for divine help.

As she cleaned and dressed the wound, she was thoughtful. "Alma, do you believe that the Lord made your hip?" The boy firmly admitted that he did, and then Amanda Smith said, "The Lord can make something there in the place of your hip; don't you believe he can, Alma?"

"Do you think that the Lord can, Mother?" the boy asked.

"Yes, my son, and he has shown it all to me in a vision!" Then she turned him comfortably on his stomach, and told him to stay in that position and the Lord would make a new hip for him. Just as she predicted, in about five weeks a flexible gristle grew over the place of the missing joint and socket. When the family reached the Salt Lake Valley, the physicians were amazed at this miracle. The boy not only walked again, he did so without any sign of nearly being crippled for life. One day as Amanda was working outside away from the home, she heard the children screaming. She ran to the house and saw Alma moving about on his legs, and everyone joined in excitement and praise to the Lord. (See Andrew Jenson, *Latter-day Saint Biographical Encyclopedia*, 4 vols. [1901–36; reprint, Salt Lake City: Western Epics, 1971], 2:792–97.)

One great blessing of The Church of Jesus Christ of Latter-day Saints is that there are programs to train up the children, programs to lift new convert adults to a higher level, programs to help mothers and others to understand their assignments of guiding Heavenly Father's spirit children along the path of righteousness—the only road to heaven and the presence of God. For example, Sister Aurelia S. Rogers was called to preside over the newly established Primary organization, which, according to Sister Rogers, would teach the children obedience, faith in God, prayer, punctuality, and good manners: "We always endeavored to impress the children with the fact that home is the place to begin to practice all good things." (Aurelia S. Rogers, *Life Sketches* [Salt Lake City: George Q. Cannon and Sons Co., 1898], p. 216.)

Eliza R. Snow is one of the greatest heroines and examples in all of Church history. Following the martyrdom of her husband and prophet, she threw herself into the Lord's service by helping in the women's organizations, comforting the sick, and assisting in the birth of babies while the Saints were heading west. She never had any children of her own, but she remains a classic example of a faithful, spirited, self-educated and God-blessed woman with a passion for the salvation of others no matter what deprivation was required of her. She lived to be an example of the believer and to promote opportunities for people to follow righteous examples. Her life was hard but rewarding in being a light among others.

In the book of Psalms we learn that in due time, faithfulness shall bring God's blessings. For example, the Lord "maketh the barren woman to keep house, and to be a joyful mother of children. Praise ye the Lord." (Psalm 113:9.)

Many years ago my husband and I met Sister Benson, companion of Elder Ezra Taft Benson, in the foyer of the Salt Lake Temple. She was leaving, and we were just arriving. I was a young mother, wife of a bishop with four children under the age of five. The temple session in those days was much, much longer. Preparing to leave the little ones for so long . . . well, you know! It wasn't easy to get to the temple, but we had made it and declared all of this to Sister Benson, a mature mother and an important person.

I will forever remember her parting words, given by way of thankfulness to the Lord: "I have six children, and I never remember a single bit of quarreling or confusion at our mealtimes around our big table."

I considered that a goal but realized that God was on her side, all right, because I could never say that about our family.

Flora Amussen Benson was an example of the believers. Her funeral on 14 August 1992 was a fitting tribute. It also provided a working plan for mothering effectively. The following excerpts include expressions from her children about what they loved about their mother, what she did that has had a lasting effect on their lives.

Mark Benson, a son, was the first speaker. Among other things, he said, "It may seem a little unusual at a funeral service to hear the hymn sung 'Do What Is Right,' which has so beautifully been rendered today by the Tabernacle Choir, and reason for the selection is that this is one of Mother's favorite hymns and personifies in so many ways what is in her heart and the teachings she has given to her children."

Then Mark quoted the various children as to what they remembered and valued in their mother. He said, "Mother has so often counseled us, 'When faced with a decision, ask first, "Is it right?"' How we loved Mother singing and living 'Do what is right; let the consequence follow. . . . Do what is right; be faithful and fearless. . . . God will protect you; then do what is right!' (*Hymns,* no. 237.)

"Beverly said, 'One of Mother's greatest qualities is her devotion to a principle. She has a great desire to always do what the Lord would have her do. . . . [That] meant to put the kingdom of God first in your life and to have absolute faith in the Lord, Jesus Christ.'"

Mark continued, "Mother had implicit faith. . . . To her children she would say: 'Just keep the commandments and all will work out all right. . . . Keep yourself morally clean. Don't be cheap. Follow the Brethren—they will never lead you astray. . . . Support your bishop and stake president,' she would say. 'They have the mantle of their callings. Put your Church work first and magnify your Church assignments. . . . Seek ye first the kingdom of God, and all will be added. . . .'

"Bonnie remembers when Mother turned down a White House invitation so she could attend her high school choir program. Bonnie later stated, "Do you know what kind of security and confidence it gives a child to know she is that important to her parents? That she is loved that much?'

"Beth reflected, 'First of all, I always felt that Mother was happy in her role as a homemaker. To be a wife and mother was always held in the highest regard in our home. There was never any complaint of being tied down or imprisoned by homemaking chores.' . . . Mother was fun—so very much fun. . . . Her sense of humor was keen and alive and sparkling.

"Reed said, 'Sometimes when we were playing games, Mother would laugh so hard she would start crying.'

"Barbara said, 'Mother never missed anything we were involved in and always supported us one hundred percent. When I was campaigning for a student government office, she helped me make posters and flyers, and then went with me to distribute them on the campus.'

"Bonnie reminisces, 'Mom made home a fun place to be. We always knew we could bring our friends over and that our yard was always available.' Mother often observed: 'There is no satisfactory substitute for a mother, and no one can take care of her children like she can. The best way to train and guide children is to be with them as much as possible.'

"Reed remembers: 'Mom knew that she was needed at home. . . . [There] was a poem we remember first from Mother's lips in family home evenings—a poem she had memorized by Edgar A. Guest: "It takes a heap o' livin' in a house t' make it home. . . ." Mom did that heap of livin' as the Lord would have her live. Thanks, Mom, for your life, for your labor, for your love, for putting first things first. We know what you want of us. You and Dad have said it for years: "No empty chairs in that heavenly home." '"

Dear readers! Though we aren't all such choice examples of the believer in Christ as her family recalls Sister Benson's being, let's think upon Mormon's words to his son Moroni: "My son, be faithful in Christ; and may not the things which I have written grieve thee, to weigh thee down; . . . but may Christ lift thee up" (Moroni 9:25).

Be lifted. Keep trying. I stood with Sister Camilla Kimball following an area conference in Texas, as she waited for her husband, Spencer W. Kimball, who was President of the Church at that time. Suddenly a young lady, pregnant with her first child, stepped away from her young husband and positioned herself before Sister Kimball. She was so overcome to be in the presence of this great lady, this beloved example of the believer, that she burst into tears. Finally she said, "Oh, Sister Kimball, my husband wants me to be exactly like you!"

Sister Kimball, ever gracious and humble, comforted the young wife: "Never mind, dear, I wasn't like this at your age either. Life is about growing up."

We can keep trying. We can keep teaching the children, helping each other. Mothers have it in their power to begin the world again, to be instruments and ministering angels to help the Lord fulfill his mission to "bring to pass the immortality and eternal life of man" (see Moses 1:39). And that means all men, women, and children!

In his dedicatory prayer for the newly remodeled St. George Temple in November 1975, President Kimball said: "We again ask thy blessing on the women in all the land, that they may accomplish the measure of their creation as daughters of God, Thy offspring. Let the blessings of Sarah, Huldah, Hannah, Anna, and Mary the mother of the Son of God, bless these women to fulfill their duties as did Mary, . . . and let the power and satisfactions of the prophetesses and all holy women rest upon these mothers as they move forward to fulfill their destinies." (*Church News*, 15 November 1975, p. 7.)

Mother: The Proceedings in Her Days

Having had a great knowledge of the goodness and the
mysteries of God, therefore I make a record of my
proceedings in my days.

—1 Nephi 1:1

Through her own records, a mother's influence is felt down the
generations. A gracious and gifted gentleman historian and I were
talking about Eliza R. Snow and her relationship with Joseph
Smith, the prayerful farm boy who grew into an amazing prophet
of God. We spoke of her clear influence on him after she became
his plural wife and moved into the home with Emma, Joseph, and
their children—among others.

The historian cautioned me, "There are a lot of myths about
Eliza. One is that she was pregnant by the Prophet and lost the
baby when Emma pushed her down the stairs. It just isn't true,"
he said.

It rolled over in my mind, "Men know a lot of things but not
necessarily when it comes to women!" However, I quietly responded, "Oh, how do you know?"

"There is no mention of this in her journals for that period."

That didn't convince me. Women in Eliza's time often did not
talk about their personal, intimate experiences. I am a journal
keeper, a woman, and a mother, and one who has searched journals, letters, autobiographies, and publications. Though a journal
or diary might be an outlet for candid personal expression, it may
not reveal a woman's deepest concerns, particularly if her record

might leave a legacy of pain. Today's media is keeping us well posted that women who are abused either as children or wives often don't openly record such happenings if they keep a diary or a journal. They are afraid to! They are ashamed to. They are too traumatized to. Women often do not record incidents that are linked with a guilty conscience or tainted with sin or mingled with inappropriate actions of others. Instead of details, some women record feelings and emotions of anguish that form the lines to read between when the journal is meant for the writer's eyes only.

Surely Eliza—true to herself as a people lifter, a spiritual teacher, a fervent poet for hymns and funerals—would not record anything that would bring hurt or embarrassment to others. That's my story anyway, and I'm sticking to it because some of the most intimate experiences and marvelous moments of my life have not been recorded. In my own heart the things I have not written are often more significant to me than the things I have!

A life recorded is a life twice lived. Even putting one's life on paper in a kind of personal code or shorthand can trigger full-blown, full color and sound remembrance of an incident or a season.

A journal used as a tool of catharsis might help . . . or hurt. That is especially true if a mother tells all about family members. A mother who labels the sinner and details the sins of family members may be overstepping the bounds of agency.

On the other hand, I recall listening to a wayward teenage boy tell me about deliberately snooping out his mother's journal so he could use it against her. Instead, he found his name in her journal and read on in fascination as his mother's writing described this son as being loved and prayed over, yearned after, and hoped for. It changed his attitude and turned his life back to appropriate behavior.

In a journal kept by author Virginia Woolf she wrote: "I have just reread my diary and am much struck by the rapid haphazard gallop at which it swings along. . . . Still if it were not written rather faster than the fastest type writing, if I stopped and took thought, it would never be written at all, and the advantage of the method is that it sweeps up accidentally several stray matters which I should have excluded if I hesitated, but which are the diamonds of the dustheap."

Perhaps the best guide in what to write is to follow the lead of the master record keepers in the Book of Mormon. Etching their thoughts on metal plates was likely slow and difficult. The records were supposed to be sacred to come forth for future generations. Space considerations and sometimes Spirit-imposed restrictions prevented the recorders from writing all but the smallest part of what they observed or felt, and so they leaned heavily upon the guidance of the Holy Ghost as to what to record. I agree with that sacred system.

Florida Scott-Maxwell was by her own admission an older woman by anyone's standards. She eased through her remaining days by keeping a notebook constantly at hand to make an account of her feelings and observations of life and its mixed citizenry. At one point she wrote, "I am getting fine and supple from the mistakes I've made, but I wish a note book could laugh" (*The Measure of My Days* [New York: Alfred A. Knopf, 1968], p. 8).

If we were to examine all the journals of all the women from earliest Church history to the present time, we would no doubt find a recurring theme: the journalists have perceived mothering more as a satisfying learning experience than as a mothers-work-from-sun-to-sun duty. There is no room for guilt or personal blame for the behavior of others when one is trying so hard twenty-six hours a day!

In my lectures on record keeping, I have often quoted from Anne Frank's diary as a now-famous reason for keeping a record: "I want to bring out all kinds of things that lie buried deep in my heart." She also lists a high personal motivation for her diary, "And now I come to the root of the matter, the reason for my diary: it is that I have no such real friend." Yet even friends don't (or perhaps we should say shouldn't) tell a friend everything!

Sister Belle Spafford, general president of the Relief Society for many years, once told me of an appointment that she kept with President Spencer W. Kimball regarding the vital charge to the women of the Church to keep personal records. President Kimball handed her a copy of an entry from his own mother's journal dated March 28, 1895. Sister Spafford read the brief entry for that day, handed it back to him, and questioned, "So, what is interesting about this?"

"It's the day I was born, and my mother didn't even mention it!"

An unknown Japanese woman kept a record of her days back

in 1897. She tells of her arranged marriage and her delight and gratitude for such a pleasant relationship as they enjoyed, each thinking "only of how to please the other." Then later she wrote in her diary:

> Now we were very happy because of the child that was to be born. And I thought how proud and glad my parents would be at having a grandchild for the first time. . . . On the eighth day of the sixth month, at four o'clock in the afternoon, a boy was born. Both mother and child appeared to be as well as could be wished, . . . but I must say that it was a very small child; for, though it ought to have been born in the eighth month, it was born indeed in the sixth. . . . At seven o'clock in the evening of the same day, when the time came to give the child some medicine, we saw, by the light of the lamp, that he was looking all about, with his big eyes wide open. During that night the child slept in my mother's bosom. As we had been told that he must be kept very warm. . . . Next day . . . at half-past six o'clock in the afternoon, he suddenly died. . . . "Brief is the time of pleasure, and quickly turns to pain; and whatsoever is born must necessarily die";—that, indeed, is a true saying about this world.

Thereafter this charming, sad Japanese girl-mother buried the ashes of two more newborn babies in quick succession. She wrote:

> I thought that, even if this new misfortune did not cause my husband to feel an aversion for me, thus having to part with all my children, one after another, must be a punishment of some wrong done in the time of a former life. And, so thinking, I knew that my sleeves would never again become dry—that the rain of tears would never cease—that never again in this world would the sky grow clear for me. And more and more I wondered whether my husband's feelings would not change for the worse, by reason of his having to meet such trouble, over and over again on my account. I felt anxious about his heart, because of what already was in my own. Nevertheless, he only repeated the words: "From the decrees of Heaven there is no escape."

She herself became ill and died within two weeks of her last child.

And if there were no word about our living, no wonder at the beginning and no understanding at the end, what's it all about? Yet if there is a record . . . Mabel Burgoyne was seventy-two when she died. At her funeral someone read the details of her birth as recorded in joy by her mother. At the end of her life here was proof and perspective about the beginning, about the reaching out and helping and brightening of her seasons. At her dying it provided a kind of resurrection, for the whole family loved their sister and each other anew in the remembering. A written line or two became their lifeline—the dry farm, the small store the mother kept in the front room of the farmhouse, the loved ones at Christmas or at daily prayer, the father's Sunday ritual, the hard times, the faithful times, the laughing times, and the struggle to add a new room as yet another baby came. It was a wonderful, rooted remembering, that funeral. There was no shriveling sadness, only a hearty gathering of reasons for being and then moving on. It seems a testimony in itself for keeping a record of the proceedings of our days.

Mother: Laugh or You'll Cry

Ask your child what he wants for dinner only if he's buying.

—Fran Lebowitz

Laugh—or you will cry! Who hasn't uttered these words of resignation, and of relief? Life does things to us, and we must find our survival as best we can. Surely nobody understands this like a mother or a person filling that assignment for a season. In the midst of tender tales, heavy doctrine, and holy charges, let us pause to be light, to giggle a bit, to consider some lines to pass along to someone else.

Years ago I read a brilliant bit of whimsy from an issue of *Reader's Digest*. It probably was penned by a man—I don't recall—but the perspective gives that possibility. At any rate, it offered inspiration for a delightful diversion of laughter—comments the mothers of great people might have made. Here are some excerpts:

Mother of Achilles: Stop imagining things. There is nothing wrong with your heel.

Mother of Alexander the Great: How many times do I have to tell you, you can *not* have everything you want in this world?

Mother of Madame de Pompadour: For heaven's sake, child, *do* something about your hair.

Mother of Franz Schubert: Take my advice, son, never start anything you can't finish!

Mother of Sigmund Freud: Stop pestering me. I've told you 1000 times already. The stork brought you.

For the leveling of their own expectations, fortunate women are taught early on that woman is synonymous with sacrifice. We include these lines by "Anonymous"—undoubtedly a woman of thoughtfulness as well as humor. I have shared it around the world in my presentations before women's organization meetings and Continuing Education lectures.

Here Lies an Old Woman

Here lies an old woman who always was tired.
She lived in a house where the help was *not* hired.
Her last words on earth were: Dear friends, I am going
Where washing ain't done, no sweeping, no sewing.
I'll be where glad anthems forever are ringing,
But having no voice, I'll be clear of the singing.
Don't mourn for me now, don't mourn for me ever.
I'm going to do nothing for ever and ever.

All right, who among us will admit to being something more than thirty-nine years old and in a holding pattern? I must now; I can't get away with anything else, given the world of mirrors that we live in. When I was young, my mother always taught me that the face you had when you were forty is exactly what you deserved. That meant skin care, of course. But her emphasis was on expression—forever frowns, drooping martyr lips, frustration furrows on the brow, eyebrows raised in an expression of constant surprise when all one is trying to do is keep awake standing up. By way of pleasant comfort as we face reality, we quote from the sardonic lines of *Warning* by Jenny Joseph:

When I am an old woman, I shall wear purple with a red hat which doesn't go, and doesn't suit me. And I shall spend my pension on . . . summer gloves and satin sandals, and say we've no money for butter. I shall sit down on the pavement when I'm tired and gobble up samples in shops . . . and run my stick along the public railings and make up for the sobriety of my youth. I shall go out in my slippers in the rain and pick the flowers in other people's gardens. . . . You can wear terrible shirts and grow more fat and eat three pounds of sausages at a go or only bread and a pickle for a week and hoard pens and pencils, . . . things in boxes. But now we must have clothes that keep us dry and pay our rent . . . and set a good example for the children. . . . But maybe I ought to practice a little now? So people who know me are not too shocked and surprised when suddenly I am old and start to wear purple.

Phyllis Diller in her prime offered many a comforting thought on how to slug through the less glorious days of our holy calling. I read too late to help me something that nonetheless made me laugh for a moment. She said that she was such a poor housekeeper that she always kept get-well cards in the drawer of the front hall table so that when the neighbors rang the doorbell she could quickly march them across the mantel! I thought of the days when our house was children riddled and the visiting teachers inevitably came the day I was *going* to clean house! But it was Phyllis who also reminded women that to clean house before children are grown is like shoveling paths before it has quit snowing.

In my burdened days of public assignment, a fabulous friend slipped a lifesaving note to me under desperate circumstances. The words themselves didn't affect me as much as the hope of the note and the caring of the friend, "Sometimes God even gives his industrious angels the afternoon to play."

To me, words are a form of action. They can influence change. Their very articulation triggers a lived experience. So mothers, who must laugh so that you won't cry, may our words give you release, if not an excuse to take some time out for you!

Mother: What's Cooking?

Civilized man cannot live without cooks.
—Oliver Meredith

M ost mothers are tied to their own apron strings. If you are in the business of mothering, you are up to your ears in food preparation—pizza delivered on order notwithstanding. It has to do with loving. You can give without loving, but you just can't love without giving. Cooking is a most giving kind of mothering. It conjures up memories and establishes ties. It fosters security and feeds the senses as well as the tissues, if you will. It is one of the most satisfying and pleasurable of mothering duties.

Cooking is *home* spelled with recipes. Each mother has her favorite recipe, and each household has its traditional feasts, treats, or staples. These are tied to time and circumstance and to the taste buds of family members.

Oliver Meredith said it well:

We may live without poetry, music, and art;
We may live without conscience and live without heart;
We may live without friends, we may live without books;
But civilized man cannot live without cooks.

It is a blind-hearted woman who doesn't recognize the real dominion a kitchen gives her. Serving up cereal daily may seem a boring nuisance, but consider the joyful perspective of M. F. K. Fisher, who geared her mothering around cooking. The kitchen was the place where everything truly important happened. Fisher, author of *The Gastronomical Me* published in 1947 (followed by a succession of popular food-oriented books), liked mothering with cooking. Her own mothering and "being mothered" memories are irrevocably linked with the kitchen. This was something that she understood about herself from earliest days when she cooked for her own family. As she grew up to reign in her own kitchen her confidence was at its peak. Intimidation and frustration might happen beyond the kitchen, but the kitchen was where food preparation reached into the realm of power. A man's home might be his castle, but the kitchen is the throne room. Fisher wrote, "The stove, the bins, the cupboards, I had learned forever, make an inviolable throne room. From them I ruled; temporarily I controlled. I felt powerful, and I loved that feeling. . . . I loved to entertain people and dominate them with my generosity."

One of the factors of the popularity of *The Shell Seekers* was the frequent detailing of family meals and guest refreshment. Many key moments in this best-selling novel were linked with food preparation. Author Rosamunde Pilcher swept the reader into Penelope's kitchen as she herbed the lamb roast for the gathering of her children. The reader longs to sit at her table and sup in such ambiance.

For twenty years Rebecca Russell Cannon—birth mother of seven, stepmother to three, grandmother to several—has been affectionately crowned Mother Christmas because of her annual Christmas Cookie Party. To an assortment of nieces, nephews, cousins—and dads, who wander in as well—she sets the tone for a happy season. In her large, attractive, and well-appointed kitchen, Rebecca has a huge round table that seats twelve, a breakfast bar with stools enough for more, plus standing room only in that fragrant kitchen. At the Christmas gathering Becky—seemingly easily and endlessly, and always happily—mixes, cuts, bakes, cools, stacks, and dispenses sugar cookies in the shapes of Christmas. Delighted guests of all ages pitch in, using the frosting pots, the candy sprinkles, and the coconut to work their creations. Cookie frosters are not limited to primary colors. Paper plate palettes extend the wide variety of colors she provides in the frosting pots. Mauve and purple and blue for bulging socks, silvery pearl for shining stars, chimney grey for Santa's boots, brick red for his suit, holly green and berry red, yellow for an angel's hair. And there is pure white and skin pink for the baby Jesus cutout.

It is wonderful fun. The conversational level among pre-schoolers, teenagers, and grandparents is charming. And civil!

Everyone is a child at Christmas in such a setting.

Everyone is an artist.

Everyone is a success, as inevitable exclamations of approval erupt over every finished cookie.

Everyone is a bit of a philosopher about the season, too. People eat as they go, sip cider or milk, and take home their own prize plateful.

This is an encompassing pleasure, and it happens in that mother's kitchen every year. Oh, yes, it's an enormous nuisance. Yes, it's an incredible mess! Certainly she is exhausted. But she's exhilarated, too. Love labors there! Each year people start asking for the date of the Christmas Cookie Party weeks before the season begins. They do not want to miss their favorite part of the celebration. How can you measure the worth of this kind of mothering? It isn't just binding one family, it's binding in-laws, neighbors, spouses, first-cousins once removed, and the inevitable near strangers seeking heart shelter in such a home.

During my senior year at college I happened to be president of Chi Omega sorority and became very close to the housemother, Mamie C. Robinson. She lived on the premises, supervising the food preparation and ambiance that helped college coeds survive tough schedules, scholarship crises, fear from frightening war. It was a tender time of lost loves, broken hearts, and hasty marriages. Also because of the war, there was food rationing and shortages. Mrs. Robinson had to be innovative with food, yet she mothered us marvelously. She always served attractive meals that comforted homesickness.

I married *my* soldier between winter and spring quarters and for fifty years have guarded Mrs. Robinson's wedding gift to me. A treasure for my time. It was over one hundred recipes written in her own neat hand and bound in a five-by-eight, black leather, six-ring binder. This was her inscription in the front:

"I hope that your house will always be full of good food. The way to a man's heart, so they say, is through his stomach. Paul Lawrence Dunbar said:

'It's easy 'nough to titter w'en do stew is smokin' hot,
But hit's mighty ha'd to giggle w'en day's nuffin'
    in de pot.'
"My interest and love are with you. May you have loads of
happiness."

That little book got me over the beginnings of family life and
steadies me now near the ending. Fifty years of use in my various
kitchens with my assorted family configurations and occasions
leave it stained and stuck with frostings, sauces, juices, fillings, pas-
tries, candies, and soufflés.

The recipes reflect the times. There is low-fat content because
fat was used for ammunition. Now with a fitness-focused generation, some of these are returning to favor.

Here are Mamie Robinson's mothering recipes for aspic and
sponge cake—or "yellow bread," as she spoke of it.

Tomato Aspic

2 T gelatin
1/2 c cold tomato juice
3 1/2 c boiling tomato juice
1 T lemon juice
1/2 tsp Worcestershire sauce
salt and pepper to taste

Soften gelatin in cold juice. Dissolve this mixture in boiling
juice. Cool. Add lemon juice, Worcestershire sauce and season-
ings. Pour into ring mold. When set and ready to serve unmold on
a round platter and fill the center of the ring with a mixed salad of
your choice.

Aspic was made from homemade tomato juice and was inex-
pensive. Another advantage to aspic was that it could be made
ahead. It was colorful. And it could be flavored and garnished to
make it the centerpiece of a Sunday-night supper or of a ladies'
luncheon for guests. So my college housemother's mothering has
been praised countless times over fifty years.

If you hold on to anything long enough, the wise ones say, it
will come back into use, style, preference. It is so with sponge
cake. It had a big day long ago and then was overshadowed by
mothers who favored whipped cream desserts and decadent

chocolate mousse or frozen pie. And then there was the introduction of German chocolate cake, leading to German chocolate everything.

But now mothers are looking to sponge cake again as a basic. New nutrition knowledge has affected our eating habits. Sponge cake is making a comeback.

Sponge Cake

6 eggs
1 c sugar
1/4 c lemon juice
1/4 tsp vanilla
1 c flour (sifted twice)
1/2 tsp salt
1/2 tsp cream of tartar

Beat egg yolks until thick and lemon colored. Add sugar gradually. Add water and flavoring. Fold in flour. Add salt to egg whites and beat until frothy. Add cream of tartar to the whites and continue beating until whites hold a peak. Fold into yolk mixture. Pour into dry, ungreased tube pan. Bake one hour at 325 degrees. Invert pan until cake is cold. (Serves 12)

Every Thursday evening Janet Booth-Palmer holds family home dinner. She is a widow with grown children who have gone their ways and grandchildren who lead chaotic school lives. But come Thursday evening, every path leads to Janet's spacious dining room where all the old favorites nobody cooks are lovingly served. The joggers, the determined trim-and-slim ones notwithstanding, the table's plentiful load soon disappears. No skimpy salad and naked chicken breast for family home dinner at *this* mother's. Hot breads, spaghetti and "secret sauce," or pork roast with pan browned potatoes and homemade applesauce are topped with "company desserts" made especially for the family. They choose from trifle, caramel cake, pumpkin pie, and more.

One memorable day, the new generation will plead for secrets from Grandmother's kitchen. When that happens to you, take it at the tide. It is a precious time. Recently Margaret Jackson-Judd's granddaughter Elizabeth was cooking in my kitchen with my own granddaughter Abigail. They're thirteen and wanted to learn how to make yummy chocolate eclairs. I loved teaching them how to make Great-grandmother Anderson's custard filling for eclairs which her mother had taught her to make for the sick and afflicted. Oh, what Grandmother Jackson-Judd would have given to hear the nostalgic sharing of Elizabeth about when she was a "little girl" visiting Grandmother Jackson-Judd. She remembers sitting like a princess on Grandmother's best living room couch where, with proper ceremony, Grandma Jackson-Judd served Elizabeth her very own, child-size, whole poppy-seed cake. "It's my favorite food memory," confessed Elizabeth.

Ginger mini-muffins would work as well for Mother or Grandmother to serve her loved ones. This is a long-time choice of Sylvia Firman's because they freeze so well and you can zap them in the microwave just when you need them. Layer them between sheets of waxed paper and freeze them individually. Once frozen they can be stored in freezer bags.

Ginger Mini-Muffins

You bake these in miniature muffin tins and top them with apple butter or cream cheese blended with frozen strawberries.

2 sticks of unsalted butter
1 c molasses
1 egg
1 c white sugar
2 1/4 c flour
1 1/2 tsp each of baking soda, ground ginger, and cinnamon
1/2 tsp each of nutmeg and cloves
grated rind of a large orange
1/4 c boiling water
4 T sour cream
dash of salt

In a small saucepan melt butter and stir in molasses. Cool. Beat egg and sugar together until fluffy. Sift dry ingredients together and add to egg mixture alternately with the butter/molasses mixture. Add the rind, water, salt, and sour cream. Blend well. Bake in greased and floured muffin tins in preheated oven at 350 degrees until puffed (about fifteen minutes). Turn out to cool on rack.

When I was a little child my mother's only sister came from Payson to live with us during her high school years. What a surrogate mother she was! She taught me all kinds of things about personal grooming and "country food for city people." She steamed her chic bob into waves by covering her head with a newspaper as she bent over a pan of boiling water, all the time chatting to me about things every girl needed to know—someday. Knowing how to make good things to eat was a top priority. There was a never-ending stream of young men who sat around our sun-room table to eat Aunt Neva's watermelon slices and spit the seeds out the window into the sandpile below. I remember thinking what a fun thing that was to do, but Mother would, of course, never allow us such tricks. Then Aunt Neva would make watermelon pickle out of the rind.

It was Aunt Neva's connections that got me my first ride in one of her boyfriends' big touring car—a rare treat. She had popcorn drizzled with caramelized sugar to eat along the way. Aunt Neva taught me to make quick-treat butterscotch dollars to take to the movies. She knew how to make the best oven-fried potatoes I've ever eaten—to this day!

She'd use eight baking potatoes, scrubbed and very thinly sliced. She soaked them in salted ice water, and just before baking she'd pat them dry between clean flour sacks (we use paper towels today). Butter—real butter—with maybe just a touch of bacon fat, was brushed on a jelly roll pan. Then the potato slices were arranged in overlapping rows and dotted with butter bits. She used salt, lots of pepper, and paprika as seasoning. The oven was preheated to 400 degrees, and the potatoes baked about half an hour until the potatoes were a crisp, golden brown.

Traditions make all the difference between one family's fare and the next. For some—ourselves included—the serving dish for a certain menu item is as important as the food itself in ringing up memories.

We cherish the Delft milk jug filled with warm milk Postum to go along with waffles Sunday evening. The blue quail English soup tureen (Quayle is an oft-used family name, after Grandfather George Q. Cannon) that we filled with clam chowder and served with our own cheesy baguettes made in our custom-created, long, skinny tins. This made a great New Year's Day menu after Christmas was taken down. There were heart dishes for Valentine's,

bunny casseroles and a deviled egg platter for Easter, and sham-
rock molds for St. Pat's day in honor of our Irish ancestors. The
seasons, the holidays, the honors children earn are celebrated with
special food and containers for *our* special family members.

It isn't that anybody's food is all that great or unique that we
relate these details. But a mother's influence and the memory of
her is linked with what is cooked in her kitchen and how it is
served at her table. It reflects the sacred memory of *home*.

When our fat family cookbook was lovingly prepared for a
milestone wedding anniversary, the introductory lines set the tone:
"The Cannon Family Collection of Absolutely Wonderful, Work-
able, Remarkable, Marvelous Recipes for Food *We'll* Never Forget."

You have your own favorite memories of meals and celebrations and the accompanying table settings. When you consider
what's cooking at your house, Mother, remember that memories
are being made to give warmth to principles taught, relationships
strengthened, and love for God encouraged.

You see, this is why civilized men and children can't live without cooks! And the more mothering the cook, the more civilized
the family.

Mothering: Make the Most of It

Men are what their mothers make them.
—Ralph Waldo Emerson

Today I stood at the counter in a fine store completing a purchase and suddenly became aware of a soft voice nudging a scampy three-year-old into appropriate behavior. The child was in the mother's arms. I hadn't turned to see what kind of people these were—I heard enough to prove their quality. The child changed from tantrum crying to petulant submission and then eager agreement. It took some time for that transition to take place, and I stood quietly and eavesdropped, for such was the beauty of the young mother's persuasion.

First, she comforted the distressed child—showing forth increased love after the discipline that swept her up into her mother's arms. Then as the child was emotionally able to hear her mother, there were words of love and of education about the beautiful store and all the nice people moving about properly so that it was pleasant to shop there. The mother firmly yet quietly talked about her own need to buy some presents for Grandma. "Isn't Grandma kind and loving to us? We want to get something wonderful for her, don't we? Can you help me decide?" A grunt, sniffle, and mumbled response from the child. "No, I can't carry you, because you are growing so big now, and we are going to have a new baby soon, remember? But we can sit down whenever you want. We could even go right now and look at the magic fountain downstairs in the mall. But you will have to cooperate. You must behave like the lovely little girl I know you really are. And if you cooperate well, perhaps you'd like to stop at the chocolate shop or the toy place, but you must cooperate, all right?"

I felt tears well up in my eyes at this mothering.

This scene was such a contrast to what I witnessed earlier in a grocery store. There I couldn't ignore an angry mother as she yanked a crying child by the arm, bouncing and dragging him along toward the door. She screamed profanities as she went. Oh, how I wanted to interfere with that kind of abuse! (It seems irreverent to use the word *mothering* in such a context.)

What kind of home did each of these mothers provide, do you suppose? What kind of adults will be spawned there, prepared there? What kind of human nature is molded under such mothering? It isn't just the comfort we feel when sweet mothering is noticed. Nor the discomfort that wells up in us as we stand helpless before the agency of a person engaged in inappropriate mothering. It's life predicted.

Home is where Mother is. What more important environment is there to provide than to share wholesome, universal, eternal values of belief and behavior with those who come within our circle of influence? This kind of environment is possible in a hut or a condo, a store, a church, or a bedside. How good this can be!

Home is a great place to live if it is a great place to live. If we understand things correctly, life is the training place for the ultimate occasions beyond the veil. May we all prepare for ourselves a proper home on earth so that we'll be ready for the stellar occasion of arriving at our heavenly home one day.

A real home has had a great deal of mothering in it, even if there is a woman alone, for she tends the garden, coaxes her houseplants with gentle talk, and nurtures the visitors who come through her door.

And if there is a tired mother, stepmother, adoptive mother, great aunt, or responsible big sister, then may God help her well-meaning heart. In our home, as you do in yours, we have long prayed for the missionaries. But I am finding my personal prayers more crowded with prayers for the mothering women in the world today. In them is the power to change the world through those they mother. Such women can mold the attitudes, soften the hearts, and stimulate the thinking of their charges. They can expose these growing ones to the plan of God and to God himself. They can teach the true worth of souls.

Mothers, teach proper manners for smoother personal relationships and acceptable behavior in a crowded, stress-filled world. Teach moral values and provide vivid understanding about the wisdom in God's commandments so that resistance against temptation holds. Teach right from wrong, and also teach best from better. Teach repentance, faith, and forgiveness. Teach patience. Teach cleanliness and refinement. Teach correct principles of the gospel of Jesus Christ. Teach prayer. It is through prayer—closeness to Heavenly Father—that spiritual discernment and security in life's situations come.

Give good gifts to your children.

We are aware of the difficulty women in emerging countries still have with child bearing, caring, and rearing. But within our own realm, motherhood has been relatively spared the anguish of needless infant mortality and the inability of meeting the physical needs of the family. However, civilization still confronts us with challenges that demand the best in and from a woman. Thoroughly modern mama is still required to love her child unconditionally, and the child is still dependent upon that anchor for emotional survival. A child who experiences this carries with it a sense of personal worth and a certain trust in personal relationships and in humanity. Such a child can grow up with faith in the possibilities the future holds, no matter what is going on in the grim happenings of politics, war, sin-for-sale, the disregard of human life— even the weird notions of men.

Mothering requires that a girl learn that she is both like her mother and yet a person in her own right. A boy must learn how different he is from Mother—from woman—but how valuable that counterpart is to him. Russell Baker wrote, "We all come from the past, and children ought to know what it was that went into their making, to know that life is a braided cord of humanity stretching up from time long gone, and that it cannot be defined by the span of a single journey" (*Growing Up* [New York: Congdon and Weed, Inc., 1982], p. 8).

Such is the value in mothering. Make the most of it if the chance is yours!

And if you are asked what it is you *do* in life, lean not upon the

professional training, the job in the marketplace, the noble volunteer work, important or necessary as such things are. Instead, put
first things first. Hype the home! Push mothering. Say something
like: "I am married with children. I build a home wherever our lot
takes us. I train up a child in the way God wants him to go. I prepare the next God-fearing, people-helping generation. I am in
partnership with God to bring to pass the eternal life of those
given to me to care for."

Mothering is such a bonus for women. Tack this quote from
Psalm 113:9 on your "don't forget to remember" board and bask
in this blessing: "Be a joyful mother of children."

Mothers Not Forgotten

Her children arise up, and call her blessed.
—Proverbs 31:28

The world is indeed full of remarkable women devoted to being lovingly responsible for other people. Many are anxiously engaged in helping children grow up right. Often women take turns mothering each other; sometimes, even, the tables are turned and a daughter mothers a mother.

I recall during a serious illness when both the disease and the medication for it had sorely affected my appearance. One day my daughter and I were walking to a large shopping mall, and I had my arm through hers as she helped me safely up the curb. A reflection on the entrance doors shattered me when I noticed it. I thanked her tenderly for walking with me when I looked so terrible. She gave my arm a firm squeeze and said, "I love you, Mom, and you have walked with me when I haven't been very beautiful either!"

Mother and mothering can perhaps best be understood in the context of a mother-daughter relationship. A mother, not diamonds as some say, is a girl's best friend. President Gordon B. Hinckley told a group of women that there was nothing more beautiful, no picture more lovely, than that of a mother with her daughters.

Much goodness in the mothering adventure is positively en-
hanced by what a mother learned from her own mother—both
while being reared at her knee and later as an adult being em-
braced in a more sisterly relationship.

Mothers are wonderful. Truly, a mother's work is never done.
Even to the grave they still yearn for those who come after them.

Mirra Jacobs Bird's funeral was crowded with people of all
ages who had loved her and had linked her gentle and charitable
ways with the hopeful, happy, and kindly experiences of their lives.
As the memorial service progressed, it became clear that she had
had a "mothering" relationship with many as she stimulated others to seek culture, read widely, think deeply, and serve glowingly
and effectively to lift the level of civilization in the home and the
larger community.

Her daughter, Julie Bird Hendry of Lafayette, California,
wrote a letter to her mother not long before she died that speaks
of that rare quality in a woman, that ability to be God's arm of
love in her mothering role:

> Dearest Mother:
>
> It is so hard being so far away from you right now. You are
> in my thoughts and prayers constantly, and I love you very
> much.
>
> You have been such a strong influence on my life—and I
> thank you for that. You have taught me courage, honesty, and
> love for our fellowmen. You've taught me to be unselfish and
> to be strong within. All these things have helped me through
> difficult times, as I know they've helped you.
>
> I appreciate so much that you are my mother. You are the
> kindest, sweetest, most gentle person I know. Happy Birthday,
> my wonderful Mother!
>
> Love, Julie

Some of the perspectives that follow will trigger your own
memories and opinions about mothers. Are you very different
from the remarkable women who responded to an invitation to
consider Mother and mothering? Their responses were heartening
and provocative. Here is a rousing, sweepingly positive outburst
on family values and their impact on society and individuals. True

experiences from a wide spectrum of women—all ages, stages, and styles. No doubt about it, remembering Mother is a good thing to do!

* * *

The Wonder-filled Institution of Motherhood

Carrie B. Henderson, St. George, Utah, combines public relations and writing as an avocation to mothering five beautiful, little children. She has published a book and is a sought-after speaker. She was born in Waukesha, Wisconsin, to Rollie and Phyllis Bestor. A convert to the Church, she married Lon E. Henderson. She is a graduate of Brigham Young University and a former star on the Cougar gymnastic team. Her thoughts on mothering follow.

Oh, the wonder of it all—motherhood! A wondrous institution with its own perpetual process of learning and growing, a school unique from any in which I have ever participated. Motherhood is a process of learning, filled with spiritual, eternal knowledge taught to us by the Great Master teacher. It is a means of learning that fills us with the wonders of eternal life, from the tiny cry of new life coming from the heavens to the shallow breath in a body shriveled with years, soon to return to the heavens. As I have allowed this institution to teach and work in my life, my wondering turns into the realization that there is no greater place than right here in my own home as a mother to learn the deep, abiding lessons of charity, unselfishness, and patience. Motherhood fills me with surprises, miracles, and tender love, but only as I permit it to be what it is meant to be.

I remember as a young girl wondering about such important things as what my baby doll, Pataburp, was going to wear: her red-checked dress with matching hair ribbon or her crocheted outfit that Oma Dorothy had made. I wondered if I should put her to sleep for a nap, or if we should go into the kitchen for a snack of apples and raisins; after all, I wanted to be her very best mother.

My, how the simple and glamorous childhood dreams of mother-hood were just that—simple and glamorous! The real school of motherhood takes you much deeper than choosing what a child should wear or deciding what to fix for a meal.

Twenty years later, I am a real mother with five little children, nine years old and under. The wonders of my life have now be-come these: How can I teach my seven-year-old who is preparing for baptism the sacredness of this covenant? Will I be able to see past those mischievous, chocolate eyes and feel a tender heart? Can I soothe the tears of a frustration only a five-year-old boy can have when his parents sell his new-found dog friend, Max? Will I notice the beauty of a "by-my-own-self" hairdo? And will I take the time to appreciate all the expressions of love as they are given in hugs tight around my legs, in spaghetti-sauce-stained kisses, or in the silent smiles of warm, transparent-blue eyes looking up at me? There is never a day without wondering how I can be so blessed to be a mother!

In the exciting little-girl expectations of being a mother, I could hardly wait—it was going to be glorious! To have a baby of my own that really cooed, giggled, and cuddled in my arms. Little did I ever imagine that it would be so wonderful because it would be so difficult. Along with the coos and giggles came cries; and many times instead of the cuddling came the independent pushing and defiance. And then they grow up! But it is through the won-der in *their* eyes that I could see the eternal glory and purpose that balance the enormous effort and time spent mothering these ten-der children from our Father in Heaven.

A reflective question from my three-year-old, Taylor, after bedtime prayers, "When will I see Jesus and Heavenly Father up in heaven, and Uncle R. Jay too?" brings motherhood into perspec-tive. Listening to my oldest daughter comment to her sister as they talked quietly before going to sleep, "I hope that I don't get too old before Jesus comes to earth, because I want to be able to sit on his lap and give him a hug and kiss," brings motherhood into focus. *That* is why I do it. *They* are why I love it!

We have an incredible responsibility to see that these children do return to Father in Heaven. Teaching them sacred things takes time and effort (especially when I have to work hard to stay a step ahead of their heaven-quickened minds). It is a task that fills me with wonder. But knowing that the rewards of doing it are equally as incredible makes each exhausting day worth it.

It seems we are in a world where we are enticed to believe that we can have anything instantly, from instant meals to immediate pleasures, from self-serving gratifications to prompt fixes. We satisfy the strongest of personal desires quickly and painlessly. The institution of motherhood teaches us differently; it requires time, hard work, and patience.

Somewhere after the birth of my fourth child and before the birth of my fifth, I began to worry about when these children would hurry and grow up so I might be able to satisfy desires for myself. I began wondering when I would be able to develop as a woman, because I was not capitalizing on the knowledge and degree I had received in college. It seemed all that I thought was expected of me as a woman distracted me from allowing motherhood to satisfy my any need or want. Motherhood became a task I would awaken to every morning only to endure; there was no joy, no teaching of principles, and certainly no teaching to share with my children. I was a mother in despair.

My wondering took me to the scriptures (thank heavens!): "He that findeth his life shall lose it: and he that loseth his life for my sake shall find it" (Matthew 10:39). I didn't have to look further than my own extended family to see women who were contented because they were losing their lives in serving their children in some extraordinary circumstances.

I have come to admire and learn from watching a sister lose herself as she nurtures two spina-bifida children; a widowed sister-in-law who was forced to lose herself rearing seven young, fatherless children; another who spends unselfish time caring for a silent, stroke-crippled mother; another, with a nonmember husband, who spiritually feeds children alone. I have observed my own mother, who has such zest and vigor as a woman because she has lost herself serving not only her four children but also thousands of students as a teacher. And I appreciate the efforts of a sister who carries the burden of mothering with financial anxiety. They don't wonder what a shame their circumstances are but allow the time and process of being a mother to fill them with maturing and love. They fill me with wonder! How could I ever complain about my position that is comparatively so easy? I feel so grateful to be able to be home, and feel for those who are unable to. But the institution of motherhood is no respecter of persons or circumstances; it can inspire and teach all of us, whatever our situation.

It was only after I tucked away my little-girl fantasies and suppressed my mature-woman selfishness that I was able to resign myself to the fact that it is the *process* and *journey* in the blessed institution of motherhood that brings peace, contentment, and joy. Living and losing ourselves in the service to our children, without seeking for worldly substitutes, brings us mothers a richness unparalleled by any worldly wealth. Is there a better institution in the world to learn patience, selflessness, sacrifice, and charity? Is there any other institution that can train us for the ultimate graduation to godhood? It is no wonder that motherhood is the highest institution of learning, filled with the wonders of eternity, for it is God's institution.

Oh, the wonder of it all! The joy of it all!

With the Help of the Lord

Barbara W. Winder has had a rich life. She has mothered her own family of children, supported her husband in important civic and Church assignments, and has mothered missionaries in Czechoslovakia and California. She is best known as a beloved general president of the Relief Society of The Church of Jesus Christ of Latter-day Saints. Her attitude about the importance of mother follows.

Not many of us begin our families with a degree in child development. Faced with the reality of family duty, we begin to acquire knowledge. What greater privilege can come than to teach children of our Heavenly Father? And when they are born into our home, the privilege becomes even more acutely our responsibility. In my day, we had the Gossell Institute with Drs. Ilg's and Ames's studies and also the ever-popular Dr. Spock to help us understand needs and solutions. However, the reflective mood I'm in tells me that following gospel principles in our lives is the thing that has the most impact for good for our children.

Let me illustrate, using Doctrine and Covenants 4:2, 5–7 as a way to focus on just a few pertinent principles: "Ye that embark in the service of God, see that ye serve him with all your heart, might, mind and strength, that ye may stand blameless before God at the last day. . . . And faith, hope, charity and love, with an eye single to the glory of God, qualify him for the work. Remember faith, virtue, knowledge, temperance, patience, brotherly kindness, godliness, charity, humility, diligence. Ask, and ye shall receive; knock, and it shall be opened unto you. Amen." Striving to live these truths daily in our homes can make a real difference in the atmosphere and quality of life influencing those who live there, as well as others who simply visit us.

"Ye That Embark in the Service of God"

Accepting calls in the Church, unhesitatingly, has been a way of life for me since I was a young teenager. I believe that any effort is small compared to the great blessings we receive from the Lord. But I have had some surprises in my life. One day I found myself sitting across the desk from my bishop-husband. "I'm calling you to be a den mother." I couldn't believe he was saying this to me! *What goes through the head of an eight-year-old boy?* I wondered. *Why couldn't he have called me to teach the Merrie Miss class?* I wondered. *After all, I was a little girl once, and I know what little girls think about and how they feel.* "All right," I heard myself responding. "But if I'm going to do it, I'm going to be happy." Then pondering, *How can I be happy doing something so foreign to me?* The answer came to my mind, *Learn how to do it.* And so I did! For eight years I served happily as a den mother, helping many young boys grow and achieve, including our own three sons. The blessings that came from serving in this assignment were many, but three stand out in my mind as being particularly helpful:

First: We lived on a farm on the periphery of the ward. We were somewhat isolated from the other families. Being the den mother brought the children to our home.

Second: Cubbing is a family activity, and even busy bishop-dads attend pack meetings. It was another way to keep our family together!

Third: Best of all, I learned to understand my boys! I learned to understand my sons, what they thought and felt, what they liked to do and how they develop—such a blessing to a mother who is expected to give guidance and direction! The Lord really does know what we need.

An interesting by-product of that service has been that each of our sons has served as an adult leader in Scouting in one capacity or another. Each son has shown patience and been helpful to his own children. The pattern has also been followed by our 4-H leader daughter, who also bore the title "Den Mother."

"Faith, Hope, Charity and Love, with an Eye Single to the Glory of God"

We don't know the end from the beginning. What we do know is who we are, why we are here, and where we are going. Every child needs to have the opportunity to know this: he is a child of God, eternal in nature, and should be respected.

"Ask, and Ye Shall Receive; Knock, and It Shall Be Opened unto You"

There is a softening influence that comes into a family when regular prayers are said, both private and family prayer. We teach one another and express the most tender feelings of love and admiration through vocal family prayers. Prayer allows the Spirit to permeate our lives.

An unexpected blessing occurred in our daughter's life, which was brought about, at least in part, because of consistency of family prayer. As a student at BYU, Susan was going through a difficult decision-making time and feeling a great deal of stress in her life. Her daily routine included a run each morning from student housing to the temple and back down the hill toward campus. The despair she felt lifted as she heard the clarion bells chime seven o'clock and begin to play the "Star-Spangled Banner." At that instant in her mind she saw us, her family, kneeling in family prayer as we had done each morning for the twenty years of her life. We prayed for Dad with heavy priesthood responsibilities, for Mom with special assignments, for missionary brothers. This morning she knew we were praying for her. Back at the dorm, a call home verified the feeling. Spirits were lifted and life was faced with renewed determination. I'm sure the task is often overwhelming, and we may slip occasionally or feel inadequate. As we persist, any degree of success brings joy.

Each child is an individual with agency to choose for himself. We can teach, and we can persuade by precept and example, but we should never force the human mind. When we have done all we can do in our human, imperfect way, I believe the Lord knows of our efforts. The person making choices becomes accountable for his own actions. We just need to keep flooding our homes with the light of the listed virtues. A positive, happy environment does make a difference.

I have a small group of friends who love to be together. Our schedules don't permit us to enjoy each other more than three or four times a year. We laughingly, lovingly call ourselves the "Mutual Admiration Society." There is such love, loyalty, and support for one another. People, young and old, thrive on positive comments. How happy we are when we remember this!

Being a partner with the Lord in teaching his children is truly a blessed opportunity. For those of you just beginning your families, "trust in the Lord with all thine heart; and lean not unto thine own understanding. In all thy ways acknowledge him, and he shall direct thy paths." (Proverbs 3:5–6.)

Motherhood, Profession of Choice

Anne Carroll P. Darger is a well-educated young mother who has been a civic leader, a member of the Junior League, and a newspaper religion columnist for the Idaho Statesman. *She currently lives with her husband and five children in Boise, Idaho. Her feelings on motherhood follow.*

When our daughter Elizabeth was finishing her kindergarten year, her teacher asked her students to state what they wanted to be when they grew up. The answers were published in the kindergarten graduation program. There was a wide range of responses: fireman, nurse, teacher, lawyer, astronaut, doctor, actress, artist, sports hero. . . . Elizabeth was the only member of her class who answered, "I want to be a mother." Actually, she said, "I just want to be a plain ol' mother," which was her way of clarifying for her teacher (Mrs. Coon later explained) that unlike other little girls in the class who perhaps wanted to be a doctor *and* a mom, Elizabeth had chosen motherhood as her *primary* career. I was thrilled to think that we must be doing something right. Because, you see, I am a "plain ol' mother."

We live in a world where value and worth are based on salary, professional position, titles, degrees, and other measurable accomplishments. This is an era when the standard philosophy is that *my* health, *my* happiness, *my* possessions, *my* appearance, *my* satisfaction, and *my* time come first. Some women who rise above the "me generation" mind-set leave their children to work out of a false guilt, because of some perceived notion that the best way to improve the world is by contributing their knowledge and expertise outside the home. Bombarded by these misguided philosophies of men, how can we help our daughters understand the exquisite joy and satisfaction; the unrivaled, infinite contribution to mankind; and the eternal ramifications of choosing to be nurturing, devoted "professional" mothers?

No one would argue that raising children requires a lot of work. Cooking dinner, washing clothes, soothing hurt feelings, teaching integrity, explaining service, wiping noses, rocking fussy babies, reading bedtime stories, changing diapers, settling disputes, baking cookies (if you really want to do it right), braiding hair, packing lunches, patching jeans, bandaging scraped knees, car pooling, grocery shopping, buttoning coats, pulling off soggy galoshes, listening to piano or violin or trumpet practicing, ironing Sunday dresses and shirts, toilet training, picking up toys, making beds, straightening rooms . . . and then, at the proper age, teaching your children to do all those things *themselves* so that they will grow up to be responsible, self-sufficient adults—it's a big job.

I used to say, "If I can teach our children to tell the truth and to read, they'll make it in this world." But I have to admit that motherhood is a bit more complicated than that. In spite of the difficulty associated with being a conscientious, full-time mother, I believe our daughters will choose this divinely ordained role enthusiastically.

Mothers need to "whistle while they work." What daughter will choose a miserable, unhappy mother for a role model? My mother (who earned a master's degree in social work and joyfully helped put Dad through college *and* law school before embarking on her life's great passion: motherhood) takes great pleasure and pride in being an excellent laundress. I remember when I was a young bride, she gently pointed out my graying wash and helped me improve my methods of prewashing and sorting, resulting in a much whiter, brighter wash. (She also reintroduced me to bleach—a marvelous invention.)

When my twin brothers were born (children numbers four and five in our family), I remember the mountains of clean cloth diapers always waiting to be folded on my parents' bed. Mother saved the folding until eleven o'clock each morning when her favorite hour of game shows came on. Getting the twins bathed and dressed and fed, the breakfast dishes slicked up, the wash started, and a few of Daddy's shirts ironed first meant that Mom could sit (the ultimate luxury for any mom) and fold diapers while she watched *The Price Is Right* (the old version with Bill Cullen), and *Jeopardy*. For Mom it never seems to be drudgery. It is certainly work, but she seems to love doing it because she loves us, and so she has always found ways to make the work fun.

Like sons, daughters need to be introduced to and encouraged to explore all of the wonderful opportunities and adventures available in this wonderful world: "anything virtuous, lovely, or of good report or praiseworthy, we seek after these things" (Articles of Faith 1:13). Furthering one's education helps broaden horizons, increase options, and provide training that can increase independence and self-confidence. It speeds us along our individual paths to godhood. Not all of our daughters may have the opportunity to marry and raise children. Many of those who do will have to support themselves and their families at some point. But it has been my experience that, given all the options and an example of a supportive father and happy mother, our daughters will recognize that while a woman has the capacity to do anything in this world, if she is fortunate enough to become a wife and a mother, that is indeed the best career of all—the most contributing, demanding, stimulating, satisfying . . . and the most fun.

I am very grateful to have parents who provide just that example, a magnificent partner in marriage who makes being a mother feel majestic, and daughters and sons who seem to be catching the vision.

Waiting Patiently

*For a warm-hearted, God-loving woman, waiting for mother-hood is one of life's hard tests. **Barbara LaPray Mason**, a fine and creative leader of girls and women, and also a wife and mother, tells her story.*

From the time I was a little girl I dreamed about growing up, getting married, and having a big family. As a child I remember playing house with all the neighborhood kids. We spent much of our time securing orange crates and arranging them into a make-believe home. I always wanted to be the mother, and Bernie Lynn Stewart was inevitably the father. Our fantasy included plans to one day remodel one of Grandpa Stewart's chicken coops and live happily ever after. Imagination and ingenuity were integral parts of our childhood play.

As I look back on those early years, I am certain that my dreams were influenced by my own dear mother. She found joy in mothering. Happiness was homemade at our house—homemade bread and biscuits, home-grown vegetables, bottled fruit, hand-made dish towels, home-gathered eggs, and even homemade macaroni and cheese. We worked hard, and we played hard. I was happy and looked forward to following in my mother's footsteps.

I received my patriarchal blessing on my seventeenth birthday. I was excited to receive a blessing from a patriarch of God. I went fasting. In my heart I was hoping and praying that my blessing would include a promise that I would marry and have children. The words, "In the Lord's own due time you will meet one of God's great spirits who will lead and direct you into the temple of the Lord," filled me with eager anticipation. I made a commitment to be good so that I would marry someone good.

That fall I went away to college. I majored in elementary education, hoping the skills and knowledge I gained would help me in my own mothering. One thing I was never told, and was surprised to learn, is that there are actually girls who attend Brigham Young University who don't date. No one had ever mentioned that possibility to me before. And I didn't date. Oh, I had lots of friends, including "boy" friends, but since dating generally precedes marriage, I graduated from BYU unwed and went off to seek my fortune.

Teaching children, my involvement with friends and family, and my Church activity gave me much happiness. I clung to the promised blessing of marriage and motherhood and continued to wait "for the due time of the Lord." I have since learned that true happiness comes as a result of giving of oneself, serving others, and serving the Lord. Being single or married does not determine whether one is happy.

Every year I grappled with where I should go, what I should do, and where the best place for me would be. The words of the song from the popular musical *Oliver* were especially relevant: "Where is love? Where is he that I close my eyes to see?" I wanted to find him. As the years passed, I continued to teach, served a mission, and concluded that the Lord was teaching me about patience. I applied to graduate school and went seeking an M.R.S. degree. I failed and ended up with a master's degree. I continued to read and rely on the promises in my blessing. The desires of my heart were to marry and have a family. I found comfort in the words of David in the Thirty-seventh Psalm: "Delight thyself . . . in the Lord; and he shall give thee the desires of thine heart. . . . Rest in the Lord, and wait patiently for him." (Vv. 4, 7.) His counsel gave me great hope.

Once while serving on a writing committee for the Church, I was asked to write a lesson on Abraham and Sarah. In preparation for this assignment I prayerfully sought to understand Sarah's feelings. I, too, knew about wanting and waiting and was learning about waiting patiently.

After teaching child development at Utah State University for several years, I was introduced to Don Mason. Fortunately for me, he was wearing rose-colored glasses. He saw me beautiful. I dated! We fell in love. When Gertie Lesser, from my home ward, heard the news of my forthcoming marriage, she exclaimed, "This will be the event of the year!" For me, "in the Lord's own due time" was twenty years. I was now thirty-seven. Don and I were married in the Oakland Temple. He was worth waiting for.

I have learned from experience that when you yearn for something and must wait and wait and wait for it, your appreciation and joy increase when your dream finally comes true. Words cannot describe the joy I felt when I gave birth to a beautiful baby girl. Tears streamed down my face as I said over and over again, "We have a baby! We have a baby!" Ann Elisabeth was a miracle. I had waited a very long time for this privilege. Discovering a mother's love was the most tender, spiritual, and fulfilling experience of my life.

I immediately resigned from my position at the university. I knew that what I wanted to do more than anything in the world was to teach my own. I delighted in telling people that I had "retired." Shortly after my fortieth birthday, Paul Joseph was born. He weighed in at nine and a half pounds. We were a happy little family. My dreams had come true.

I know that Heavenly Father answers prayers. For years I had been praying for a family. I was reminded of these prayers as I was passing out Doublemint gum and singing, "Double your pleasure, double your fun, two little babies are better than one." We were having twins. When Susan Christine and James Christopher were born, our "little" family became a "big" little family. With four under four, my status quickly changed from "retired" to "real tired." Our joy was full! So was our car. Don went searching for an affordable vehicle that could transport four occupied car seats plus a proud mother and father.

In retrospect, I thought I had learned a lot about patience in my waiting years. I readily admit that I didn't learn enough. My patience wears thin, wavers, and sometimes is lost before the children even leave for school. Patience requires effort, it takes practice, and it is replenished with prayer. Sometimes humor and creativity help. One year I picked, polished, and protected two of our near-perfect pears to enter in a small country fair. (We live where it's almost too cold to raise pears, and I think our crop consisted of not more than a dozen.) Just before I was to leave, I discovered tiny nibbles in my irreplaceable prize pears. I was upset! I swallowed my pride and entered them anyway with a little sign that read:

The Masons Are Raising Pears and Children

I need to be reminded daily that my children and their feelings are more important than possessions and how others may judge me.

Being a mother isn't easy. It's challenging. It's busy but rewarding. Patience is a key to successful parenting. I learned once that those who do the best job of parenting are those who enjoy it more. (See A. Lynn Scoresby, *In the Heart of a Child* [Salt Lake

City: Bookcraft, 1987].) I'm trying to patiently enjoy. I am grateful for the sweet memories of wanting, wishing, and waiting on the Lord. He truly granted unto me all the desires of my heart.

Essay on the Life of My Mother

Eudora Widtsoe Durham, wife of the late G. Homer Durham of the Presidency of the First Quorum of the Seventy, writes a wistful remembrance of her mother and her mother's mother. She lures us into the lives of prominent and fascinating people of the early Church years in the Salt Lake Valley. Eudora herself has great talent and charm and has reared an outstanding family of her own. She is comfortable in the academic world, having been the daughter and the wife of university presidents. This is her remembrance of the mothers in her life.

My mother lived a life that she made happy in spite of many challenging experiences and the prevailing circumstances of her life and times.

Let's start at the beginning. Mother was the first child born to her parents. Her mother was seventeen-year-old Susa Young Dunford, and her father was Dr. Alma Bailey Dunford, one of Salt Lake City's first dentists. They named their daughter, born 24 February 1874, Leah Eudora Dunford.

A second child was born to Leah's parents, a boy named Bailey. Leah's parents became estranged from each other soon after Bailey's birth.

In the hope that "absence makes the heart grow fonder," the young father accepted a missionary call to go to the Hawaiian Island Mission.

Susa enjoyed her freedom from her husband, and, as she was still young in years, she enjoyed "making the rounds" of many parties. There was a difficult divorce from Alma Dunford while he was still on his mission. It was very sad, as I have been told, and the judge gave Leah to her father, while Susa was given her baby son.

Leah's father subsequently married Lavinia Clayton, and their life was happy. It was blessed with many children and congeniality between "Aunt Vinnie" and Dr. Dunford.

Susa also found complete happiness in her second marriage, this with Jacob F. Gates, by whom she had eleven more children, several of whom died in infancy and early childhood. She and Jacob accepted a mission call to Hawaii, where three of her growing family were born. Missions were longer then than now. The Gateses lost their two eldest sons to "diphtheritic croup" there, much to their sorrow.

As a child, Leah hardly knew her mother. When Leah was a teenager and her mother was living in her mother's apartment, Susa arranged with Dr. Dunford to have Leah live with her for two summers (Leah's maternal grandmother was Lucy Bigelow Young, the twenty-second wife of Brigham Young). Mother and daughter found they dearly loved each other. Dr. Dunford was happy to let Leah spend some time with her mother.

Leah subsequently attended the University of Utah. She studied hard and loved every minute of her work. Homemaking and nutrition were her favorite subjects. She sang with the choirs and participated in school activities. It was no surprise that as valedictorian of her class of 1896, she was asked to be one of her graduating class's commencement speakers. Of these occasions, Karl Maeser allegedly said that he was glad young women wore long skirts, for then those in the audience could not see the shaking of their knees!

During these years, Leah was sought after by many young men. However, she did not wish to become serious with any of them, remaining just friendly.

The Courtship Begins

While living with her mother, Leah spent the summer after her graduation enjoying life. Susa, now established as a Church writer and editor, learned that Harvard University in Cambridge, Massachusetts, allowed women to attend its summer sessions. Her interest in genealogy took her there, and she was invited to dinner at the J. M. Tanner home.

J. M. Tanner had taken a group of six or seven young LDS men to study at Harvard and other prominent Boston institutions, the first from Utah to study there. These youths roomed and boarded with the Tanners, and their rent allowed Mr. Tanner to afford to attend Harvard himself. At the dinner Susa attended, the young man who was asked to pray was John Widtsoe, an LDS convert from Norway six years earlier.

His prayer was so sincere and intense that Susa made arrangements before she left that night to meet and become better acquainted with young John Widtsoe. As her acquaintance grew into friendship, she told him of her daughter Leah. Would he give her a picture of himself for her to give her daughter Leah? She would have Leah send one of herself to him. Susa hoped the two of them could meet, fall in love, and marry.

On her return to Utah, she painted a glowing picture of the young man. Leah was not too impressed and said to her mother, "Well, if you like him, I am quite sure I won't!"

The following summer, Susa organized a group of young women to travel to New York City and attend the Pratt Institute of Home Economics. Leah was one of the young women, and naturally they were to spend a few days in Boston. There they were chaperoned by Maud May Babcock, a young woman socialite from Philadelphia who was a bit older than they were. Maud's parents were not at all happy that Susa Young Gates had become her friend and had invited her to Utah to teach at the University of Utah. Maud May Babcock brought her specialty to Utah. Her field was basketball. She brought basketball to Utah! Later she changed fields and became a professor of drama and speech at the university.

Her parents became so concerned about her mingling with Mormons that they sent her brother to Utah. He had just graduated from Temple University Medical School in Philadelphia. St. Mark's Hospital was just opening that year, and Dr. Wayne Babcock was the first intern they hired. Meanwhile, Maud May Babcock had found the gospel, and Utah remained her home.

The two weeks the young women spent in Boston prior to their New York studies at the Pratt Institute were a dream come true for John and Leah. Despite Leah's initial fears, the two got along famously. They explored Cambridge and Boston and shared their hopes and dreams for the future. When Leah left for New York City, each felt desolate without the other.

For Leah and John, there followed three years of letter writing—also a misunderstanding or two. Leah discovered that John would always take care first of his mother and maiden aunt who lived in Salt Lake City. John also had a younger brother who was on a mission in the Society Islands in the South Pacific.

At last everything seemed possible to the sweethearts, so with great faith they planned their marriage for 1 June 1898. They felt sure they could manage, and they did!

Leah and John's Life Together

After their wedding in the Salt Lake Temple, presided over by President Joseph F. Smith, the young couple left for Goettingen, Germany. John had received a scholarship from Harvard towards his Ph.D. degree in chemistry. In addition, John and Leah borrowed money to support them for the duration of John's studies in Germany.

Leah's mother asked them to take Leah's younger sister Emma Lucy Gates to Germany with them in order that she might study the piano. They were happy to do this. It gave the two sisters the opportunity for companionship. They constantly relied on each other and shared memories of the homes they had left and to which they would someday return.

Emma Lucy's teachers in Germany discovered her marvelous coloratura soprano voice, and Lucy became an opera star, remaining in Germany as a top artist until the outbreak of World War I. She became known as "Utah's greatest operatic singer" as well as "Utah Nightingale" and "Utah's first lady of music." She spent four years as a prima donna in German opera houses, singing over fifty roles. She later married attorney and member of the Council of the Twelve, Albert E. Bowen.

John and Leah's first child was born in Goettingen, a daughter they named Anna. John received his doctorate, and, saying good-bye to Lucy, they went to Switzerland for more graduate study. England followed for six months, and while there they were notified of a professorship available at the Utah State Agricultural College in Logan, Utah.

They moved happily to Logan and began about a sixteen-year sojourn at the college in which John moved from professor to president of the school. He was also becoming well known nationally and internationally for his knowledge and research in dry farming.

They wanted more children, but Leah had great difficulty in bearing children: she lost several premature babies, and others died in their early childhood years. They had hoped for ten or eleven sons and then two or three daughters. Instead, they were allowed to raise only three of their seven children, two daughters and one son. No one could have had more wonderful parents than they were.

In 1916 John was offered the presidency of the University of Utah. There they stayed until John was called to be an Apostle of The Church of Jesus Christ of Latter-day Saints. While an Apostle, he was "loaned" to countries and communities that needed his scientific knowledge to help meet their water demands. He was expert in dry farming and using water wisely. He remained a General Authority until his death in 1952.

Leah was first of all a devoted and loving wife to her husband. She adored him and trained her children not to marry unless they felt the same as she did. She taught us that marriage is an eternal bond that gets better with each passing year. Her example was elegant, and our desire was to choose as wisely as she did and start the eternal path as righteously as she did.

Her belief in the eternal view extended to her children, who would also be a part of her eternal family. There is a joy in belonging. I think that belief guides to better things while on this earth.

Following John's calling as a Church leader, he was sent to England, where John and Leah and their youngest child lived for seven years. They helped the young missionaries and the newcomers in the Church to truly live and understand their beliefs.

They traveled a great deal during the seven years. Their German language abilities from their early years came in handy. Church groups were in almost all of the European countries, and it was necessary for them to visit the missionaries and the groups living this new gospel.

The friendship Leah gave to so many was delightful to see. Her friendships grew and remained over the years.

She set an example as a student's wife, then as a university professor's wife, then as the university president's wife, and finally as a General Authority's wife.

She was an example of goodness and generosity wherever her paths took her. The world became a little empty without her counsel.

A Granddaughter's note: In today's pop nomenclature, Leah's childhood family experience likely could be termed dysfunctional, yet my memory of my Grandmother Widtsoe is of a gracious, intelligent, thoughtful, mature woman who saw life in a positive light. She transcended the challenges of her early life and the loss of many of her children and was certainly a role model for me. I admired in particular her profound faith in her chosen religion and her tolerance for others whose faith might not be as strong.

I might add that Leah Dunford Widtsoe was her distinguished mother's literary collaborator and confidante. She returned from the Pratt Institute in 1897 to accept an appointment at BYU. Like her mother, she was a writer and lecturer and collaborated also with her husband, who had a distinguished career as a scientist, writer, and administrator. She was an excellent embroiderer, played the guitar and sang in her youth, loved to dance, enjoyed her garden, and had beautiful clothes. She believed that good nutrition supported fitness, good health, and well-being. She didn't care for refined sugar, nor did she like Bolsheviks. She taught me to draw and provided materials for my creative expression throughout my youth. Her home was elegant and continental with sun porches, plants, oriental carpets, and walnut furniture. I have my own insights into her nature based on stories that she told me, and likely my sister and brother and cousins would have their versions. However, this is my mother's story, and I find the topic an interesting one. Leah D. Widtsoe was a remarkable woman.

Mother, My Teacher of Life Lessons

Virginia I. Peterson has been a loving mother and wife, a successful schoolteacher, constantly upgrading her skills in education by extensive graduate study. She sang with the Mormon Tabernacle Choir for over twenty-five years and now is over the 186 women of the choir, doing wardrobe and scheduling choir costuming for the Sunday broadcasts and the concert tours. She writes poignantly of her mother's influence that culminated with the circumstances of her death.

When I think of my mother, Ruth, my eyes swell with tears and my heart beats a little faster. I realize my still tender feelings about my angel mother. She was my teacher of life lessons, my security, my healer, my confidante, my example, and my best friend. She instilled within me an eternal love of Christ and his teachings.

I'm sure that toward the end of her life, Mother realized that she had not completed her task of teaching her daughter vitally needed future skills, for it was in her last year that she taught me the most influential lessons.

Mother had always been so vibrant, energetic, and skillfully organized. She made the most of every minute. Her large brown eyes twinkled as she eagerly began her usual busy days. She was small—five foot three inches—and she wore a size-four shoe. Complimenting her dark eyes was her satin-smooth olive-colored skin and her black hair, which curled naturally around her face.

Then one year the holidays were over, and the all-too busy festivities of preparation seemed to have taken their toll. Mother complained of exhaustion and of an elevated fever. Perhaps it was a winter cold. The thoughts of the spring sun warming the world would surely be the cure. Antibiotics had not been discovered. Her knowledge and gift of healing had not worked.

An examination by her doctor found it necessary to have further tests in the hospital. Father's business took him out of town often, so it became my responsibility to take Mother for the tests. It was difficult for me. I was young, in my mid-twenties, barely learning to care, nurture, and be a mother. My own children, Bobby and Ann, were only two and a half years old and eight months. I was trying to balance feedings, naps, and the usual children activities with their additional needs. I began to have a sense of "something is terribly wrong."

After four days of testing, Mother was diagnosed as having a tumor in her abdomen. Surgery was immediately necessary. Mother went in for the scheduled operation. The lab reports told us that it was the fastest-growing type of cancer. It could snuff out her life within two weeks. But Mother, in her love for life, lived for the next ten months.

Illness and suffering were new to me. I was frightened and timid about my own ability to accept what was about to happen. With my sister and brother living away and Father working on a project out of state, I knew that I would have to meet the challenge of caring for her. Mother was not yet finished with her lessons of life. If I could endure this trial, I still had much to learn.

So what did I learn in the final year of Mother's life?

I learned that each person is given an inner strength to recognize and do what he or she is called to do, pleasant or unpleasant, happy or heartbreaking.

I learned the importance of boiling a hypodermic needle for twenty minutes and how to give a shot to help Mother's nausea and calm her anxieties.

I learned, when her soon-fragile body seemed to be dehydrating, how to administer an intravenous feeding, and I learned how quickly life could come back into her life.

I learned how frightening such an illness could be. Having just turned fifty-eight years old, Mother was still comparatively young and had such a will to yet live. She didn't want to be alone. In her valiant way, she never complained or talked about it but instead bravely faced her verdict in what seemed to be silent acceptance.

I learned that I could never repay all the marvelous, compassionate friends who showed their love and concern by their contributions. This was a life lesson that I would become aware of in the coming years. I would become sensitive to those in need throughout my life. And in doing so, I would add a link of deeds to an ongoing chain.

I learned how important touching and hugging could be, like giving her a warm bath or brushing her hair. As I gave her a nightly rubdown, I could not only observe her body becoming more relaxed but also see how this disease was ravaging her.

I learned how important quality time was with her. We held hands, we giggled, we cried. She shared her cooking secrets. She instructed me on making Swedish buns and dumplings and many other specialties. I listened intently to her carefully chosen advice as I knew she was preparing me to live on without her. On days of fear and terror, I held her frail body in my arms, our hearts beating in tandem as we tried to make plans for the future days and weeks . . . something to hold on to.

I learned how to be her ray of sunshine. I soon realized how important it was for me to be upbeat, happy, and cheerful, even though I was crying on the inside. A bright approach gave us both a lot of strength.

My sister from California came to spend time with Mother and to give me some relief. Mother was so happy to have her there. She planned and organized the days. On Friday, 11 November 1955, Mother planned the weekend meals. She called Table Supply and placed the grocery order, as she had done for so many years. The weekend dinners were taken care of and the Saturday events were planned. That evening Aunt Cassie and Cousin Helen came to visit. Mother was calm and alert. The pain was diminished and she hadn't had an IV feeding for several days, although her body was dehydrating and she was so thin. But she seemed at peace.

That night, I prepared her for bed, gave her the usual tender rubdown, refreshed her bed, fluffed her pillows, hugged her, and told her how much I loved her. I said that I was grateful for my good life, the result of having a good mother. I tucked her in bed, kissed her forehead, and told her I would see her in the morning. She closed her eyes and went into a peaceful sleep, a sleep from which she would not awake. I strongly feel that she had willed herself to go. Father, Lorene, Wilford, and I were with her early Saturday morning when we realized her sleep was final. By eight-thirty A.M., 12 November, Mother drew her last breath. She was gone. She was at peace—no more pain, no more nausea, no more fear.

What did I learn from this? I learned that there are worse things than death. The worst thing to me was remembering her sick with the effects of this insidious, fatal disease. I had known her ill for ten months and had known her as a well, energetic, vibrant, life-loving woman for all my other twenty-plus years. The last year overshadowed the healthy years. We had lived through it. I had survived my tragic loss. Death was sweet compared to the suffering.

Following her funeral and the ensuing months, I became bitter. If God had needed her, as I was consoled by many, why didn't he take her earlier? Why did she have to suffer so with pain and starvation, as evidenced by the transparent skin that loosely covered her body?

I was yet to learn another lesson. This was the power and effectiveness of positive thinking. I had served night and day for a year to give my mother the best care possible in her own home, where she felt secure and happy. Our combined positive thinking prolonged her life, giving us both added strength and joy in diffi-cult circumstances. I know that the time spent with Mother was a great blessing and honor.

And finally, I learned the importance of prayer. I uttered many prayers, knowing this was my source of strength. I acknowledged blessings—past, present, and future. I felt presumptuous that God would have time for my pleadings. But, in his infinite wisdom, he seemed to know our needs and sent us comfort, courage, and peace.

Although Mother was not healed or cured, she and I recog-nized the blessings of God's eternal plan of salvation. We spoke of the order of the world, the laws of nature, and our beautiful sur-roundings. We spoke of the many years prior to her illness and of our good life, individually and as a family.

In the thirty-six years this lovely mother has been gone, there has never been a day that I have not felt her influence or her close-ness. Her imprint was clearly etched upon my heart. In life she taught me well, but in her final year of life and in her death, she walked with me through the peaks and valleys. It was then that I learned some of the most important of life's lessons. These have been the hallmark of my philosophy of living, which I hopefully have passed on to my children.

A Letter to the Mother and the Father of a Special Child

Brookie Peterson lives in Bountiful, Utah, but has traveled ex-tensively throughout the world with her husband, H. Burke Peterson of the First Quorum of the Seventy. She also served as matron while her husband was a temple president. Together they reared their family of five daughters in Arizona. She is the author of A Woman's Hope. *Now there are twenty-one grandchildren. Brookie considers being a mother and grandmother as an ultimate blessing in her life. She feels the utmost compassion for mothers who find themselves having to face formidable problems in their families.*

The following is a letter she sent to a mother and a father who were parents of a newborn son. It is an attempt to share some of her

understandings about children who are born with special problems—
problems that change the life of a family. Brookie has had no personal
experience of such problems in her family but has listened carefully
through a long lifetime as other mothers of such children described the
tugs at their heartstrings and the ways they sought to heal them. Per-
haps many of us may one day face this kind of trial in our own fami-
lies, whether with children or among grandchildren. Most of us have
friends who have to battle with such a challenge. Our understanding
and compassionate caring can lighten their burden.

Dear Roberta and Preston,

Your father called today and told me that you have a beautiful
new baby son. He also told me that he has Down syndrome. I
know that you have long looked forward to his birth as the fourth
in your family. Discovering he had this problem must have been a
difficult shock for you when you had no prior knowledge of it.
Just last year when one of our daughters was expecting her sixth
baby, it was thought for a few weeks that her baby had the same
condition, so I have a little inkling of what you're feeling. (For us,
however, it turned out to be a false diagnosis.)

I have many good friends who have lived with what you are
now facing. One of them, a Relief Society president, has a devel-
opmentally disabled son, and she has a genuine understanding of
some of the difficulties. Her son is twenty-nine now, so her view-
point is broad as she has had numerous close friends over the years
among the parents of the other children he has gone to school
with. She says there is at first a time of pain, anguish, and disap-
pointment, but parents grow into the realization that he is part of
the family now, and they must go on from there.

At length, and often before too long a time passes, they come
to realize the blessing he can be in all of their lives. Without excep-
tion this has been the feeling of those I know who look back on
that time of first acknowledging the problem and all that has gone
on since. They say the child has blessed their lives. It would be
hard to perceive that at this point, but perhaps their perspective
will bring some comfort.

Recently, we were in Germany at a servicemen's conference.
On Sunday we went to dinner at the home of one of the coun-
selors in the stake presidency. They have six children, and the

youngest, about seven months, has Down syndrome. It was very touching to watch his brothers and sisters with him. No child could be more loved nor have more fun than they were all having together. I know the older children are learning to be kinder, more sensitive to others' needs, more loving toward each other as they help with their little brother's development. His mother says that he has training and therapy already and that the day before we came, the German nurse who was working with him muttered to herself, in German, "He is not that far behind!"

Remember that he is as individual as your other children are, that he will have likes and dislikes and desires just like anyone else. Early intervention and education is very important and helpful. The more the other children help with the baby, the more they will have an interest in him and his progress. You can explain to them that you don't love the baby any more than you love them, but that for an interval you will all have to spend more time taking care of the baby.

My friend says that because of the tremendous strain on the mother and father, they can learn to rely on each other. Seldom did her husband and she both get deeply discouraged at the same time, so whichever one was having a hard time, the other could help.

Another thing she learned when she was going through her experience was that others want to help and sometimes have a lot of difficulty expressing themselves tactfully. Because of this, sometimes they make mistakes that can hurt you in the things they say or the way they say them. For example, one friend said, "I'm glad you had this baby. The Lord knew I couldn't handle it." She said she had to learn to allow for their ineptness in communication and remember their good motives.

I remember reading an article about a young man, born without arms, who told the story of what happened shortly after his own birth. His father and mother and one set of grandparents were sitting in the hospital room weeping when his little Mexican grandmother came in and, observing the whole situation, said something to this effect: "You must stop feeling this is a tragedy. I don't know the reason, but I know that Heavenly Father sent this baby to our family for a purpose. We must rejoice that he found us worthy, and we must try to learn what is to be accomplished by us to fulfill his purposes." I thought it was remarkable that she could have that kind of spiritual insight and wisdom so immediately after and in the midst of their common trial.

There is the story of a blessing given to a mother by her stake president. Prior to her request for a blessing from him, he had observed how wayward her husband and children were and had judged her, to his later shame, to be lacking in good judgment and in child-rearing skills. He learned through the blessing that he was inspired to give her that she was quite the opposite. It humbled him to discover in the blessing that she had been "a valiant spirit in the premortal existence who had volunteered for hazardous duty on earth." She had been given the responsibility to work with a husband and children who were precious to the Lord notwithstanding their waywardness, and "if they were to have any chance at all it would be because of her Christlike patience and long-suffering with them." (See Dr. Carlfred Broderick, *One Flesh, One Heart: Putting Celestial Love into Your Temple Marriage* [Salt Lake City: Deseret Book Co., 1986], pp. 50–51.) Perhaps you two were chosen to raise this little one because of your rare compassion and sensitivity.

I have another friend who has had three severely handicapped children out of her total of six children. At birth the children appeared normal, and the parents did not find out until a few months after the birth of each that the child had a cerebral-palsy condition. She is able to say now with honesty, "I'm glad Heavenly Father didn't heal Heather when she was six months old and we pleaded for him to cure her." One reason why is that Heather's life has blessed so many other lives. The mother can't believe how many people both near and far are helped by the lives of her handicapped children. When I told her that I talked about Heather to young people in Sweden, and some told me it had a real impact on them, she said she was not surprised; it had happened so often.

Recently I wrote something down that I had observed:

Sometimes we think those who are most talented offer the most in this life. Rather often, I think, it is not so. One day in sacrament meeting I was sitting near a family. On the back row were the father, mother, and youngest son, David, age twenty-nine, though his mental maturity is about age three. On the row in front of them were the parents' other son, his wife, and three children. In my mind I compared the brothers. The older has served a mission, married in the temple, and is raising a family. The younger can't read, has never held a job, will never marry or have children, but he has accomplished great good in this world—not only to his family but to others who observe and learn from him and his family. One may be stronger, a better leader, more socially adept, yet we must never underestimate what the other can accomplish. It may be much more than we would suppose. I know David has made tremendous contributions to a wide circle of people.

I hope that none of the things I have said have been inappropriate or have given you distress in any way. If they have, please forgive me and recognize that I am like many others you will find who want very much to help but don't quite know the right way. Of course, I don't fully understand what is helpful, because though I have lived much longer than you, I have never experienced what you are now encountering. I do know that for a time one must mourn for what has been lost—for the child you expected—before you can adjust to the child you received. Notice I didn't say *love* the child you received; I know you already love him, but you may need time to adjust to an unknown and unexpected situation. There is a lovely little allegory that has moved me to tears on more than one occasion. It was written by Emily Pearl Kingsley and appears annually in the "Dear Abby" column. It clarifies the emotions that may arise and is enlightening, I think:

Welcome to Holland

I am often asked to describe the experience of raising a child with a disability—to try to help people who have not shared that unique experience to understand it, to imagine how it would feel. It's like this . . .

When you're going to have a baby, it's like planning a fabulous vacation trip—to Italy. You buy a bunch of guidebooks and make your wonderful plans. The Coliseum, the Michelangelo David, the gondolas in Venice. You may learn some handy phrases in Italian. It's all very exciting.

After months of eager anticipation, the day finally arrives. You pack your bags and off you go. Several hours later, the plane lands. The stewardess comes in and says, "Welcome to Holland."

"Holland?!?" you say. "What do you mean, Holland? I signed up for Italy! I'm supposed to be in Italy. All my life I've dreamed of going to Italy."

But there's been a change in the flight plan. They've landed in Holland and there you must stay.

The important thing is that they haven't taken you to a horrible, disgusting, filthy place, full of pestilence, famine and disease. It's just a different place.

So you must go out and buy new guidebooks. And you must learn a whole new language. And you will meet a whole new group of people you would never have met.

It's just a different place. It's slower-paced than Italy, less flashy than Italy. But after you've been there for a while and you catch your breath, you look around, and you begin to notice that Holland has windmills, Holland has tulips, Holland even has Rembrandts.

But everyone you know is busy coming and going from Italy, and they're all bragging about what a wonderful time they had there. And for the rest of your life, you will say, "Yes, that's where I was supposed to go. That's what I had planned."

The pain of that will never, ever, ever go away, because the loss of that dream is a very significant loss.

But if you spend your life mourning the fact that you didn't get to Italy, you may never be free to enjoy the very special, the very lovely things about Holland. (*Deseret News,* 29–30 October 1990, p. C3.)

I hope that through this experience you two will become closer to one another and learn to more truly depend on the Lord and to trust in him. Know that he will not forget you but will strengthen you in all ways. As you face your challenge together, you have the opportunity to become "spiritually minded" (Romans 8:6) and be a resource to countless others whom you can lift with your empathy and spiritual guidance. You will be remembered in our prayers, and we send you and your family our love.

Mother—Life's Finest Blessing

*Emma Rae McKay Ashton, wife of Conway Ashton, is herself
an exemplary mother of five, grandmother of thirty-four, and great-
grandmother of three choice spirits. She has served in the women's organizations of the Church on the local and general levels. She is an
echo of her famous mother in loveliness, intelligence, and devotion to
the Lord and his work. What a delight to read some of her remem-
brances of her remarkable mother, Emma Ray Riggs McKay, wife of
President David O. McKay!*

On the children's eighth birthday, Mother gave them a party
to which they could invite their friends for well-planned games,
cake, and ice cream that she had prepared.

On Saturdays, she took her young family shopping with her.
Often the excursions ended with a silent movie starring John
Bunny, Fatty Arbuckle, and the Old Maid, or a Big Bill Hart cow-
boy show, features she knew they would enjoy.

The Barnum and Bailey Circus was an exciting annual affair
the McKays seldom missed. The wise parents suggested the children work for their show admission by digging dandelions out of
the front lawn. They paid them a cent for every ten they dug. The
evening before the intended matinee, their father, with a twinkle
in his eye, would say, "Which would you rather do, keep the
money or go to the circus?"

One of them invariably would say, "Keep the money," but
being outvoted would accompany the family to the anticipated
event.

When her children were young, Emma Ray McKay served as
president of the Ogden Fourth Ward Relief Society. Determined
to make a success of this position, she bundled her baby in his car-
riage and pushed him, making personal visits to the sisters of the
ward and inviting them to attend the Relief Society meetings. Her
diligence was rewarded. The membership increased from twelve to
ninety. Later, she was asked to be a counselor in the stake Relief
Society presidency and traveled to the various wards on a streetcar,
again taking her children with her. When she found this to be a
hardship as her family increased, she was released from this position. She next served as a teacher of the Religion Class in the

Ogden Fourth Ward, then as president of this organization for two or three years. Being able to accompany her children every week proved to be more compatible with her home situation. To her, home and her children came first.

Through this organization and the Sunday School, her children received valuable experience appearing before an audience. She directed two children's plays and a duet, "The Lord Is My Shepherd," in which one of her boys sang the alto part. She always insisted upon hearing her children give their talks aloud at home before they spoke in the meetings.

"Let me hear it," she urged.

"No, I don't want to say it to you."

"Yes, come on. Just let me hear it."

Her coaxing netted results. She corrected mispronounced words and coached them on standing up straight, speaking loudly and clearly, and in memorizing the thoughts they wished to convey. Under no circumstances would she allow them to read their talks.

These wonderful parents built family traditions. Christmas at the McKay home was (and is) a joyous holiday, with everyone participating in the fun. Secrets were whispered behind closed doors, for surprises were part of the excitement of Christmas. Many of the gifts given were handmade, secretly worked on weeks before the December holiday. Santa Claus was real; so were brownies, who reported to Santa each child's daily behavior. The Christmas tree was truly their own—and well earned. The two oldest sons, with their father and uncles, obtained permission from a property owner to cut trees in Ogden Canyon. They climbed the mountain in the snow, tramped from one evergreen to another until they spied the prettiest and bushiest, chopped it down, and hauled it home. Since it was always too big, it required much sawing and shaping to fit the corner of the living room. Mother always let the children trim the tree. She showed them how to string cranberries and popcorn and how to drape them in artistic loops from branch to branch. Red and green balls with silver tinsel and a star at the top completed the traditional decoration. She made each of her children a red and white felt stocking that Santa, on Christmas Eve, filled with nuts, apples, candy, and a surprise in the toe. She even filled them again with goodies on New Year's Eve, the present being a new toothbrush for each family member.

Summer traditions, too, were formed. The children looked forward to the close of school because summer vacation was spent on the farm in Huntsville—riding horses, jumping on the hay from the beams in the barns, and enjoying a daily dip in the delightful old swimming hole. For Mother, the change meant careful planning and organizing, washing, ironing, cooking, and packing. Each summer the Model T, or current automobile, was piled high with supplies of food, clothing, and bedding. Life on the farm was hard, with few modern conveniences, but for years she made the best of the situation and made a happy home for her loved ones.

Home and her children still came first. She continued to maintain a high level in the spiritual and cultural atmosphere in the home. Keeping standards high was as natural as breathing. With complete unselfishness she guided those around her.

"Won't you take the easy chair?" "Let me help you." "You may have my share." These were her familiar phrases. In her daily routines she manifested her selflessness. Every morning she rose between five and six o'clock to prepare a nourishing breakfast for her busy husband and children; every day, with no word of complaint, she kept warm the midday meal, even though it might be served any time from twelve-thirty to two, depending upon her husband's appointments; in the evening if he was detained, she would feed her family but wait for his return to have the evening meal with him. "I know it isn't pleasant for Daddy to eat alone," she would remark.

She was not only patient, loving, and understanding but also beautiful in form and feature. One person remarked that she was the most beautiful bride she had ever seen. In her appearance and in her housekeeping she was always neat and, though soft-spoken, was cheerful with a sparkling sense of humor.

She said, "Life's finest blessing is the ability to find joy in doing something for somebody else." She lived as she taught.

In the April 1942 *Relief Society Magazine,* she wrote, "True prayer springs from the sincerity of the soul. To be successful in rearing a family to be true Latter-day Saints in every sense of the term, parents must be sincere. They must do as they pretend, perform what they promise, and really *be* what they appear to be." (P. 254.)

Mother had many honors bestowed upon her, but she loved best the tributes from her children. How we loved her!

Beth Harmon Tidwell Potts—
My Mother, My Heroine

Claudia T. Goates is executive director of the International Association for Families. She is the mother of eight children, the grandmother of six grandsons (and a granddaughter on the way), and the wife of Dr. Delbert Goates. Her mother was cruelly, needlessly murdered. Claudia's memories of her relationship with her mother are heightened by this fact. Tenderly she remembers the power of her mother's mothering, to the benefit of the reader. Her story follows.

The most beautiful and meaningful lessons I learned from my mother were not things she necessarily set out to teach me but rather those things she did that impressed me as I was forming my own value system.

Mother loved to read because she loved to learn. She loved to work hard at cooking and cleaning and then crawl into nice clean sheets and savor a good book. I noticed the things she read were always uplifting—the scriptures, classical literature, or anything else that would improve her as a person, such as a book on maintaining a positive mental attitude. I learned to love the scriptures and other good books because I sensed the joy they brought to her.

When we were children, all we had in our home in the aftermath of the Depression was a book of scriptures and a set of encyclopedias. Our limited supply of books didn't discourage her from reading to us. She spent hours reading to us from the encyclopedias. Whether it was the words she read or the warmth and security I felt as she held me in her arms as she read that had the most positive impact on me, I am not sure. Perhaps it was just the fact that she loved to read that gave me such a continual desire to learn. The books and articles the Spirit prompts me to read have become my wisest friends and greatest source of comfort in times of emotional need, so her example has served me well.

Another great lesson I learned from observing my mother's life was how magnificently she handled adversity. She raised five strong-willed children without much help. We adored our father. He supported us financially very well and was one of the kindest, most loving men I ever knew. However, he was not often available to help with the family, which created an additional burden for Mother. She never faltered and seldom complained; she just raised us alone and did it well. When my father lost his life in an automobile accident, she still had four children at home. Again, she shouldered the hurt and just worked harder at raising the children—really alone now without the emotional or financial support of a husband.

About twelve years later Mother remarried, only to lose her new husband in another automobile accident. This time she was present in the vehicle and was severely injured in the accident. For weeks she lay in intensive care in a coma with severe head and body injuries. The doctors told us that if she lived she would be a vegetable and that our visits to her wouldn't help, because she didn't even know we were there. We knew differently because all of the monitors on the life support equipment she was hooked up to began to dance when we walked into the room. We knew at some level she did indeed know we were there.

Mother knew she was loved, and she wanted to live; miraculously, she fought her way back from a three-month coma. When people asked her how she was doing, she whispered the same words we had whispered in her ear day after day for weeks and weeks, "I'm getting better every day." And she did. She had to learn to walk again and talk again, but she recovered well enough to live in her own condo. She insisted on taking care of herself in spite of the fact that she lost nearly all of her eyesight, had poor balance, and had fallen and injured herself on more than one occasion.

My admiration for her is indescribable as she fought her way back. Even finding that tragically her second husband had been killed in the accident that had put her in a coma, she never became bitter but continued to live and appreciate the things she did have—particularly her children, grandchildren, and the gospel. Her life ended as heroically as she had lived it—in a beautiful spot. She loved to be at the family cabin in Oakley, Utah. She had gone to "Tiede's Tranquility" on 23 December 1990 with my sister, Kaye Tiede, her husband, and their two daughters. Two escaped parolees entered the cabin and shot my sister to death. Mother jumped up to help Kaye and in the attempt was shot to death herself—leaving four children, seventeen grandchildren, and six great-grandsons to remember the lessons she taught. Her lessons of courage, faith, determination, love, and a positive attitude will never die but will be passed down to future generations as a living monument to her life.

My mother taught me to love to read, think, pray, and find answers to heavy questions. The question I continually asked myself as I watched my mother suffer was, Why do good people have to experience so much affliction? Her life had been one of constant adversity. Watching her suffer has been a significant part of my own adversity. One of the blessings of adversity I saw was that it makes one "real"—it removes masks, it helps erode pride and puts one more in touch with one's spiritual self. Adversity is the refining fire that purifies us and prepares us to meet our Maker. I have watched it happen; I have experienced it. Mother was certainly prepared to meet her Maker.

Memories of My Mother—
Marie Jones Barlow

Arlene B. Darger is the wife of Stanford P. Darger and the mother of five children. They have fifteen grandchildren. She graduated in psychology from the University of Utah after her children were grown, and went on to work as a psychologist for the Utah State Handicapped Children's Service. She filled a mission with her husband to Frankfurt, Germany, where he served as executive secretary to the Europe Area Presidency. Shortly before her mother died, Arlene finally mothered her own mother. Theirs was a loving relationship, and her memories of life with her mother follow.

It's been almost four years since she closed her eyes and happily drifted off to her eternal glory and my father's waiting arms. And yet thoughts of her are still in my mind almost constantly, and I find myself thinking, *I will call Mother and see if she would like to go with us.*

The mere mention of the Salt Lake Temple or driving to or past it opens the floodgate of memories. It was there that my father, her beloved eternal companion, suffered his fatal heart attack that left her alone for the next twenty-one years. So typical of him, he had dropped her off at the entrance to the temple, to save her steps while he parked the car, and was walking up the sidewalk toward her, a temple suitcase in each hand, when he collapsed. The doctors said he was gone before he hit the ground. She always considered that to be her personal commission from him to do temple work, and during those twenty-one years she attended the temple all day two or three days each week. Those twenty-one years saw her perform the temple ordinances for nearly nine thousand souls who were patiently waiting for this work to be done. Even when she was very fragile, this sweet commitment rejuvenated her and gave her the will to endure to the end.

The doctors said that her husband's death should not have been a surprise to her—he had known of his weakening heart condition for a long time. As a matter of fact, the day before his passing he had made a point of paying off the latest bills that had just come and telling her where all the precious papers were, as though he were methodically checking off his list. But he had never told her the seriousness of his condition. You see, she had been a "kept" woman in the most loving sense of the word. My father was from the class of truly gentle men who always ran ahead and opened doors, held her arm for support, and would never allow her to carry anything, not even the new babies. He would help her get settled into the seat, then lovingly lay the precious bundle in her arms.

My mother had a lot to learn after his death in order to become independent, and learn she did. And she did so with class, never complaining or being demanding of those in the family but instead rising to every occasion and playing out the drama of her life like the great actress she could have been. Only in the last few years did she admit to being tired and lonesome for her sweetheart—and anxious to be together with him again.

Of course, challenge and hard work, and even loneliness, were not new to my mother. She had accepted my father's decision to be a traveling salesman and be away from home from Monday to Friday every week, for that would provide a better life for their six little children than any other work he was qualified to do. So every Monday morning at five o'clock he drove away from our house, not to return or be in touch with us again until one or two A.M. the following Friday night. Car phones, of course, were not even a dream back then, and long-distance calls were made only in the case of an emergency. So Mother was left virtually home alone with the demanding, unrelenting, and often unrewarding responsibility of raising six children through the hectic infant years, the critical teen years, and on to college and marriage. All six of the children have had happy and successful temple marriages, which is some indication of the effectiveness of her and their efforts.

It was really only after I became a mother that I realized fully how terribly alone and lonely my mother must have felt. My struggles in raising our children were much easier when I could discuss them each night with my husband and share the concerns and the burdens, the decisions and responsibilities, the day-to-day joys and triumphs. Some of my fondest early memories are of my mother sitting in the white, wooden rocking chair that my father had tied underneath with wire, with all six children gathered at her feet as she would read our favorite stories from the scriptures or another chapter in *Thundercave*. I have memories of her kindly setting out a sandwich and glass of milk for the men who would knock on our back door and ask for something to eat during the Depression years. And she could never turn down a door-to-door salesman. We had sets of encyclopedias, a beautiful hardbound set of music books, a set of wonderful silver-stone pots and pans, and always big bags of pine nuts in the fall when the Indians would go selling door-to-door, their heavy gunnysacks full of pine nuts slung over their shoulders.

My mother kept a very close relationship with her mother, often helping her with her work and at the same time doing some of her own. I remember streetcar trips clear across town to Grandma Jones's house. Mother would shepherd all six of us onto the streetcar, along with all of our bags filled with laundry and whatever it took to keep little ones happy in those days, and Grandma Jones would meet us at the corner of her street an hour or so later, and we would skip and run together to her house. Grandma Jones just walked, because she had a wooden leg. Her leg had been amputated above the knee some years earlier because of what they called tuberculosis of the bone, but that did not affect her disposition. She sang and whistled cheerfully as she rubbed the clothes up and down on the scrub board, wrung them out by hand, then carried them outside and hung them on the line to dry. I'm sure my mother learned her great attitude and received much strength from her mother, and she surely inherited her mottoes, Work with What You've Got, and Whatever It Takes, We Give.

My mother was a magnificent manager. She and my father decided they would never go into debt, and they saved for the things they wanted until they could pay for them with cash. I remember how proud they felt when they were able to pay cash for those purchases. My mother bottled hundreds of quarts of fruit each year that were state-fair quality, but the two items that she was most famous for were her green-tomato jam and of course her deer-meat pie. I have yet to eat anything that compares to the rich flavor of her wonderful deer-meat pie. My father loved to go hunting each year and was nearly always successful in bringing home a deer. My mother bottled the meat and made it into stews and those marvelous pies. Mother was also a champion bread baker. Warm bread, right out of the oven, was a regular treat when we came home from school.

And of course there was the sewing. With four little girls her treadle sewing machine was seldom still, especially when we grew up into young ladies. There were special dresses for every occasion, costumes, formals, and finally wedding dresses. In later years, as granddaughters came along, they too became grateful recipients of Grandma's sewing artistry. For years she made each one a flannel nightgown for Christmas. She sewed outfits for their missions and items for their bridal trousseaus. Then she turned to quilts and afghans. Each of her grandchildren received one of Grandma's beautiful afghans or quilts to take to college, mission, or marriage, and to treasure always.

Mother's frugality and careful planning made it possible for each of us to have all the lessons and special advantages that she and Daddy felt were important and had never had. She encouraged us and sat with us while we practiced. We all knew she expected us to do our very best, and we tried to live up to her expectations.

Christmas was Mother's special time, with beautiful new outfits she had made for each of us and matching outfits for our dolls. She would decorate the house with red and green velvet ropes and white paper bells. Daddy always cut our tree himself, somewhere in his travels, and brought it home fresh and fragrant. The tree was not always perfectly shaped, but by the time Daddy finished drilling holes in the trunk and inserting and wiring in extra branches it was as perfect as nature and man could make it. Daddy put on the lights and Mother put on the long, shimmering silver icicles, each one meticulously placed so that the end result was a vision of breathtaking beauty. Mother started preparing for Christmas in January, making the gifts, nightgowns, quilts, afghans, and so on, and by September she would have them all laid out on the guest bed, carefully wrapped and tagged. The card on each gift would say, long after my father was gone, "With love, from Grandpa and Grandma B."

During the years while my father was traveling and absent from our day-to-day happenings, Mother made every effort to keep him a part of our lives. Her conversations with us were always, "Daddy and I . . . ," and she would often respond to a request, "We'll wait until Daddy comes home." She told us stories about his travels and the fine people he met. We always prayed for his safety, but it was not until one Saturday morning when we went out to the garage to see his badly damaged car that we realized how critically important our prayers were and felt that truly our prayers were being heard. Fortunately he had not been injured, but he told us how he was driving along in the black of night and suddenly realized that the road was no longer beneath him. Apparently a road crew had removed a section of bridge that spanned a thirty-foot chasm and had failed to leave any reflectors or lights to indicate the break or to block the road. By the time he was aware of this it was too late to stop, and he could only pray that he would somehow reach the other side. He told us that he could actually feel the Lord with him, and it was as though some power carried that car and set it down on the other side. I think it was then that we all began to believe in miracles.

Because of my mother's example, I have the most profound respect and gratitude for the power of prayer. I also have the deepest respect, admiration, and gratitude for my mother's indomitable courage, for her steady faith, and for her positive, confident approach to life. I can imagine that she had to remind herself each day that these were the circumstances of her life, and she could make of them heaven or hell; that each of the children would take his or her cues from her, and if we saw fear, or anger and resentment, or hopelessness and resignation, these forces would affect all our lives in a powerful, negative way. I imagine that she had written on her heart, "Do all that you can, and don't worry about the things you can't change. Pray always and be believing."

With all her devotion to helping us develop our talents and interests, she did not neglect her own. She loved the theater and performed major roles in several plays at theaters in Salt Lake City. She gave many years of service in the Church. But her greatest service was to her husband and children, who all rise up and call her blessed.

For all of the above—for her never-ending support and encouragement; for her failing to be critical or doubting of my ideas, decisions, and efforts, even when she might have been; for the love she showed in her persistence in helping her children to live up to her expectations; for all the memories; and for so much more, I shall be eternally, enormously grateful.

I must add that there is another mother whose memory is also very dear to me, who touched my life in a very significant way, and for whose unqualified acceptance and inspiration I shall also be eternally grateful. That magnificent person is my husband's mother, Eva Williams Darger. But that is a whole other story.

Remembering Mother

Blanche Miles is an artist and a seamstress. Her skills have afforded her a unique opportunity to serve as a textile conservationist for the Museum of Church History and Art and for the Beehive House in Salt Lake City, Utah. She studied cultural arts at Brigham Young University and in private classes but credits her mother's home training for her most important knowledge. Her recollections follow.

My mother. Just the words bring a flood of feelings that warms my being. Hardly a day goes by that I am not reminded of her in some way. Often it is only a reflection in a mirror, and I think, *Oh, there is my mother!* As I get older, I begin to look more like her, but I do hope that some of her inner qualities are reflected through me, too.

Mother, Hannah Ellen McKell Bowen, was not college educated, but she had a great deal of common sense and wisdom that aren't necessarily gained with a degree from a university.

One of my earliest memories of Mother is at the sewing machine (she made many of the family's clothes). She stopped her sewing to teach me an important lesson: tell the truth. Evidently I had told a little fib, so she told me the story of "The Little Boy Who Cried Wolf." The boy tended the villagers' sheep on the hillside. Because he got bored and lonesome, he called "Wolf!" to which the villagers responded by coming to his aid—only to find there was no wolf. He did this several times when there was no wolf among the sheep. When a wolf finally did come among the sheepfold and he cried for help, the villagers didn't believe him, and the wolf killed many of the sheep. The moral: If you want people to believe you, tell the truth.

Mother was kind and compassionate. To offend or deliberately mistreat another person was a great offense in her sight. Befriend the less popular, don't exclude one from the group, dance with the boy who asks even though he is not your favorite, don't cancel a date because you get a better offer later. As a child in grade school I was invited by a friend to spend a weekend at their ranch, but the neighbor girl whom we both played with was not. Mother suggested that I not go, because Louella would feel very bad about being left out. I did not go. Somehow I could easily put myself in Louella's shoes.

In our family when we were given a responsibility, we knew we had better be dependable. If we had a talk to give or an assignment to fill or if we had given our word, we had better come through. There was no faking illness or dreaming up a limp excuse. I must have been about eight years old when we lived on a farm in Shelley, Idaho. At the time we didn't have any cows and got our milk from a corner country store. I was to get the milk and had plenty of time before dusk. However, a friend across the street promised she would go with me "in a minute." The minutes stretched to an hour or more until the sun was getting low, and then my friend changed her mind! I knew I was in trouble because I still had to get the milk. I found myself walking home in the dark—a pretty scary thing. I did not delay again.

Our family lived in modest circumstances, but we always had

good food and comfortable beds to sleep in. One of my fondest memories is of my sister and me climbing the stairs to our bedroom, snuggling under clean sheets, and smelling the fresh air. In the winter in our cool room we had a hot water bottle at our feet. I can still remember the delightful smell of those sheets after they had been hanging in the sunshine. You can't get that smell from a clothes dryer!

Mother was an early riser, even when she stayed up way into the night before finishing a sewing project for one of the children. I can't remember her ever lingering in bed unless she was ill. She was forever working, it seemed to me. She sometimes cooked three meals a day for threshers during harvest time. The men loved to sit around her table because Mother was such a good cook, and they could always have seconds if they desired.

During the fall season I thought the "bottling," as we called it, would never end. She put everything she could from the garden into bottles. Like a little squirrel, she took care to provide for her family during the winter season. After it was all done, what a glorious sight to see all those colorful bottles of pickles, jams, jellies, chili sauce, fruits, and vegetables on the shelves! I remember feeling put upon to have to help with all that work but quite triumphant and satisfied with our industry when the "fruits of our labor" were displayed in the fruit room.

My parents often visited the sick, the lonely, the widow or widower, and the elderly, but they never went empty-handed. They always took something from the Bowen kitchen to cheer and brighten the lives of these people. When Father retired from the farm in Burley, Idaho, he and Mother moved to Provo. Although she did not need to cook so much anymore, Mother couldn't seem to stop. She shared her excess with family and neighbors. She became known as "Cookie Bowen" to the children in the area, who soon knew where the cookie supply was. She was delighted with the name.

During World War II, Mother wrote dozens of letters to the men serving in the war, and she always wrote to the missionaries, knowing how welcome mail from home would be, especially during the holidays. She received dozens of letters in reply.

During these war years, there was a German prisoner-of-war camp near Burley. Since many of the men were in the service, there was often a shortage of help in the fields at critical times.

Dad used some of these prisoners on his farm. These Germans might have been our enemies, but they were also some women's sons and husbands. On a hot day Mother would often take them lemonade and cookies. She hoped that someone was being kind to our men in some foreign land.

Mother was a woman of good humor, quick to laugh and enjoy a good joke. She had her share of trials and heartaches, but she never lost her sense of humor. Even in the last months of her life when she was so ill, she tried to smile. On one of my visits to her in the nursing home, I said, "How are you today, Mother?" Her reply was so soft that I couldn't hear her. After asking a couple of times, I put my ear down near her mouth and heard her say, "I'm croaking!" This was an expression from her era that made us both laugh. I learned from her and my father that humor and laughter can make a rocky road much smoother.

Her faith was strong. It saw her through two serious illnesses that brought her close to death. It comforted her when Dad was almost killed when in his truck he was hit by a train, and when her children were gravely ill. God was her friend and companion.

Mother was the embodiment of a homemaker. She was content and happy with her role in life. She didn't aspire to more.

How is it possible to measure up to your mother? I keep trying, but if ever an angel lived on earth, it was my mother.

Mother, the Spirit of Our Home

Mary Elen Bennett Belnap lives in Jakarta, Indonesia, with her husband, Dr. Dean Belnap. They have also lived in Great Britain when they presided over the English East Mission. She was president of Associated Women Students before her graduation from the University of Utah. Her list of civic activities parallels her life as a mother of six children and a grandmother of twenty-two. She is the daughter of Emily Higgs Bennett, beloved leader of Church women, and her essay that follows includes gratitude for her mother and her mother's mother.

Is there anything that compares to the challenges, joy, responsibilities, heartaches—but always satisfaction—of motherhood?

I've had the thrill of seeing a newborn calf, of raising triplet
lambs in our kitchen and feeding them by bottle. I've seen a duck-
ling hatch from an egg kept warm for weeks by a faithful mother.
I've grown a beautiful zinnia from seed. All these events have
helped me to be patient and watchful and to appreciate growth
and development. But nothing has been more exciting and rewarding, or more challenging, than my forty years as a mother of
six, mother-in-law of six, grandmother of twenty-two, and wife of
one. And as Annie said in *Annie Get Your Gun,* "I ain't down yet."

Let's start at the very beginning—my beginning. As a two-
year-old with a four-year-old brother and a one-year-old brother, I
moved to the house where my father still lives, and has lived for
sixty-one years.

I was the oldest girl, but in the next ten years our family grew
to four girls and four boys. Growing up was exciting, but I never
appreciated fully what a great blessing my parents, and especially
my mother, were to me. Maturity and my own experience in
mothering sparked the realization that as a child I really had it
all—a loving family, a father and a mother who truly loved and
served each other, who never quarreled, who always trusted each
other, who loved each child, who had faith in Heavenly Father and
the gospel of Jesus Christ, and who expected a job well done but
rarely criticized if it wasn't.

Mother was the spirit of our home. This fact was poignantly
brought back to my memory not long ago when in California I
visited a friend from high school and college whom I hadn't seen
for twenty-five years. She came from a divorced home and had visited our home on many occasions. Before she even asked how I
was, she wanted to know about my parents. I told her about my
ninety-one-year-old father and about my mother passing away at
age eighty-eight. Then she rehearsed many of the interesting
things about Mother that I hadn't thought about for some time—
Mother's small loose-leaf notebooks with important items ranging
from lists of what to take on a two-week trip to organizational papers describing the whereabouts of items in the attic (a place she
hadn't climbed into since we were children, but a place organized
and kept that way by us as we did our annual cleanup). My friend
asked about the large world globe in the study where we spent

time visiting and talking about world events. She wanted to be sure the Swedish hand-painted cabinets were still above the alcove in the kitchen and detailed the joy she felt in coming to our house.

My friend spoke of my mother creating a loving and peaceful home. Even though Mother was not always home—for sometimes she was in New York (Daddy was manager and later president of ZCMI), and other times she was at a convention or on assignment for the YWMIA, where she served for over seventeen years on the board or in the presidency—her spirit permeated the home. To help maintain her influence, she sent all of us cards whenever she traveled the world.

Marmee (her mother and my grandmother) lived with us. She too had been on the YWMIA general board for many years. She was a great help to all of us—especially when Mother was away. I was always amazed at her ability to work hard all day—getting meals, washing, cleaning, and then going to her desk at night to do her genealogy. Her willingness to be so helpful had a quiet influence on all of us. Actually, I had two motherly examples. Marmee had been a widow since her early thirties. My mother remembered the day that her ailing father called her to his bedside and said, "Be a good girl and care for your mother." Soon after that, when she was only eight, he died. She did just as he had asked and took care of her mother and younger sisters while Marmee went to work to support the family.

Mother remained happy, optimistic, and helpful in making the best of life. Money was short, but the family was long on togetherness and support. I remember her telling us about the two dresses she had in college, but by changing the collars and cuffs she made the dresses seem like many. (This lack of material possessions was in sharp contrast to what we possessed when I was growing up.) Through the hardships, she developed a great sensitivity and love for those who needed help or who were less fortunate than she.

Mother was a writer—she worked hard to finish her university degree in just three years and to then acquire a job to help support her mother and sisters. Her fresh approach to her ads and articles always brought letters of commendation and favorable comments from people unknown to her as well as from friends. Long after all of us had left home, Mother began teaching mother education in Relief Society. Then, in her early seventies, she was asked to pen short articles in the monthly Garden Park Ward newsletter.

In addition to Mother's fresh approach to life through her writing, which started early and brought her the honor of being valedictorian at her high school graduation, she had a fresh approach to cleaning. We were all involved in a thorough job of it, especially for Christmas. Nothing was left unwaxed or needing polish. In fact, I learned to love cleaning because I set my goals according to the symphony I would put on the record player. I programmed myself to finish the job by the time the records were finished. (My favorite was Mozart's Fortieth!)

When home, Mother lived in a clean "model coat," which snapped in the front and was easy to get in and out of for nursing or hurrying to shower and dress for the next event.

Mother embroidered her initials on all her hankies and always carried one for us if we needed it. She also sewed in the label "I belong in Harold and Emily Bennett's little house" on her towels, sheets, and the like. Few were ever lost!

After I was married she came to visit us every year while my husband, Dean, and I lived in Virginia and later in London, where we presided over the England East Mission.

I was never conscious that I was receiving an advanced degree in motherhood, but I did, for I learned to clean, work, care, complete a project, be kind (and hopefully sensitive), trust in the Lord, be nonjudgmental, and be well rounded. Mother wasn't much for sports, but she encouraged us in all facets of life. We learned to appreciate good music, good books, good theater, and good friends.

From Mother I learned that home is the laboratory of life, the true training ground for motherhood. Most of the knowledge and values I brought into my new home forty-one years ago were acquired around the dinner table—our nightly family home evening. From 6:30 to 7:00 P.M. for the twenty-two years that I lived there, we ate together, even if Mother or Daddy were away. During those hours I cemented my love of culture, economics, gospel ideals, family love, and leadership traits.

I feel great love and gratitude for my mother's life and what she gave me. As I labor to "mother" my extended family, I sense the awesomeness of the responsibility I have to support and sustain them and to carry on the legacy that my mother left me, a legacy of total devotion to righteous principles of giving, sharing, and loving, as evidenced by her example of service, commitment, and work.

I remember the day before she passed away. I walked her up and down the hall at home, telling her again that the doctor said that she must keep active. So she persisted with me. I never dreamed she would be gone the next morning. We were all there at her bedside when she stepped from this life into the next. We were all reminded during those times of something we all knew quite well, for she told us, "A mother's love does not die." I am quite sure that in the shadowy places of mortality that lie ahead for us, Mother will reach forth her hands to guide us safely through. She always said, "Unto whom much is given, much is required." I'm trying. Thank you, Mother.

On Goals

Evalyn D. Bennett is the wife of a retired law professor, Wallace R. Bennett. She is the mother of five children, grandmother of eight children, and writes a monthly newsletter for scattered extended family members. She is a popular speaker and booster for young mothers gathered together in a variety of causes. Her list of goals has the delightful quality of keeping life for harassed mothers on an even keel. Lest mothers take themselves too seriously, Evalyn has written this bit of humor.

As a young woman approaches marriage and child rearing, she sets up some lofty goals, hoping to make her newly established cottage a little bit of heaven. As the years roll by, these specific goals have to be reevaluated and changed with the changing times and circumstances.

My goals twenty years ago included these:

1. Keep an immaculate home that would be an ideal setting for the Spirit of our Heavenly Father to dwell. To do this, organize my work into daily routines with weekly, monthly, quarterly, and yearly tasks.
2. Read the newspaper daily and at least one excellent book a month so I can become well informed about the world around me.

3. Prepare well-balanced, attractive gourmet meals, experimenting with at least one new recipe a week.
4. Bear many children, who will be well dressed, well pressed, and well behaved.
5. Keep an optimistic outlook on life. At the end of every week try to evaluate what created in me good feelings or frustrations.
6. Tell my husband once a day that I love him.

The first two years of our marriage, before children, were like a fantasy. I was so organized, inventive, and adorable. We ate such creations as cordon bleu and capon under glass. Our discussions were stimulating, and the house was hygienically spotless—not a thing was out of place.

Then came the first child. With the demands of burping, changing, loving, bathing, rocking, washing, and praying, some of my goals needed to be modified. I had to give up my immaculate home. My revised goals now read:

1. As I pass a table, blow hard on the top to rearrange the dust.
2. Put the vacuum in the middle of the living room first thing in the morning so that anyone calling will think that sometime soon I intend to get the debris from the floor.

Then came the second child. With the demands of burping, changing, loving, bathing, rocking, washing, and praying, some of my goals needed to be modified. I had to give up my book reading. My revised goals now read:

1. But not my newspapers. Ann Landers's advice column is as good as a Psychology 101 class providing me with deep insights into human relationships. If I can glance at Dr. Rex Morgan on the comic page once a week, I can keep up with the latest medical technology.
2. To keep well informed, I rush to the door when I hear the mailman to discuss some pertinent problems: "Has the garbage been picked up down the street yet?"

Then came the third child. With the demands of burping, changing, loving, bathing, rocking, washing, and praying, some of my goals needed to be modified. I had to give up my elaborate cooking fests. My revised goal now read:

1. Serve one hot dish a day. This means that if I serve hot soup for lunch, I can get away with peanut butter and jelly sandwiches for dinner. When I do find an extra hour and want to ease some guilt, I cook up a storm—meat loaf, mashed potatoes (from packaged flakes), Jell-O salad, and Popsicles. The children always ask, "Who is coming to dinner?" or "Is it Thanksgiving already?"

Then came the fourth child. With the demands of burping, changing, loving, bathing, rocking, washing, and praying, some of my goals needed to be modified. I had to give up well-dressed children. My revised goal now read:

1. Dressed. If the diaper is hanging around the knees by noon, my neighbors know that I pinned it properly earlier in the day. I haven't seen the bottom of my ironing baskets for three years, and I don't see any relief in sight.

Then came the fifth child. With the demands of burping, changing, loving, bathing, rocking, washing, and praying, some of my goals needed to be modified.

1. My goal no longer reads, "Keep an optimistic outlook on life. At the end of every week try to evaluate what created in me good feelings or frustrations." It now says, "Keep my voice down until noon. At the end of the week, count my children to reconfirm I have five. Check my mind to see if I have lost it. Check my varicose veins to see if my legs will carry me through another crazy week."

My last goal, "Tell my husband once a day that I love him," now simply says, "Try to speak to my husband once a day." With Cub Scouts, Little League, preschool, Virginia Tanner dance lessons, violin lessons, PTA board meetings, United Fund drive, Primary Blazers, Relief Society visiting teaching, University Women's Club, chicken pox, roseola, hepatitis, Asian flu, and tonsillectomies, I feel lucky to call out to him as we rush past each other going in and out of the front door, "Golly, dear, I am over-drawn at the bank again."

Twenty years later, my goals are really summarized in the phrase, "Sustain life and endure to the end." And a good pair of support hose certainly helps.

* * *

Aren't women wonderful? Aren't mothers marvelous? Isn't the wide variety of mothering techniques interesting to witness? Distinguished women's reflections about their mothers and their mothering experiences surely give us something to think about.

Mothers and others who are mothering, the praise of the prophets is upon you; husbands, sons, and fathers love you. They may even envy the secret smiles you receive from the children. And God, whose plan you function under, has this to say through Ezekiel, "As is the mother, so is her daughter" (Ezekiel 16:44).

There is something for mothering women to feel in reading the beginnings of Jesus, the preparation of Mary for this incredible motherhood. And there is something to learn at the end of the Savior's life when "there stood by the cross of Jesus his mother. . . . Then saith he to [his] disciple, Behold thy mother!" (John 19:25–27.) The Savior's last words of concern were for his own mother. Surely, that concern was part of her reward.